Newspaper Money

Fred Hirsch and David Gordon

NEWSPAPER MONEY

Fleet Street and the Search for the Affluent Reader

Hutchinson of London

For Maggi
D.S.G.

To the memory of Donald Boggis

Sometime sales representative
for the *Daily Express* for
northern Essex
F.H.

Hutchinson & Co (Publishers) Ltd
3 Fitzroy Square, London W1

London Melbourne Sydney Auckland
Wellington Johannesburg Cape Town
and agencies throughout the world

First published 1975
© Fred Hirsch and David Gordon 1975

Set in Monotype Plantin

Printed in Great Britain by Flarepath Printers Ltd
St Albans, Herts, and bound by
Wm Brendon and Son Ltd, Tiptree, Essex

ISBN 0 09 123920 6 (cased)
ISBN 0 09 123921 4 (paper)

Contents

TABLES

CHARTS

Preface

This is not a treatise on the British press but a brisk discussion of what we see as a neglected influence on its shape and content. The book is a joint product; the foundations were laid by Fred Hirsch, and most of the new investigative work was done by David Gordon, but the ideas as well as the text have been thoroughly discussed between us, and we share responsibility for the end product. Neither of us is clear precisely who hit on the final shape of the remedial scheme we propose in Chapter 7. The thought that if there is one thing worse than writing a book oneself it is writing a book with someone else occurred at a number of stages; but in writing the preface only a rosy glow remains.

We have had help from many people. In Fleet Street some newspaper managements were very helpful – at Times Newspapers, IPC Newspapers and the Financial Times in particular. These groups have allowed us the scoop of publishing for the first time their detailed profit and loss figures. Other national newspapers were less keen on disclosure. It is a pity that the Royal Commission will be forced by the needs of confidentiality to aggregate profit and cost figures, thereby obscuring the significant differences between newspapers.

For the chapter on Europe we had the benefit of information and advice from Stephen Hugh-Jones, Roland Huntford, Peter Norman, Michael Van Os, Mary Venturini, and Jackie Alo of the Newspaper Publishers Association; but responsibility for what has appeared remains ours. The research underlying Chapter 5 was done by Jeremy Andrews while an undergraduate

Preface

at Christ Church, Oxford. Circulation figures are published by courtesy of The Audit Bureau of Circulation.

Laurence Whitehead and Brian Barry of Nuffield College, Oxford, and Alastair Hetherington of the *Guardian*, made many useful comments on an earlier draft of part of the material; Nicholas Faith was characteristically generous with his criticism.

We would like to thank Polly Giles for typing, Richard Natkiel for the charts, Ian Swanton and Jenny Brown for their help with figures, and Ruth Hirsch and Maggi Gordon for their contribution to the whole production process. The index was prepared by Timothy Hirsch. David Gordon is grateful to his colleagues on *The Economist* for their forbearance while he was dividing his time between the paper and the book.

January, 1975.   F.H.
                                                            D.G.

1 The newspapers your money can't buy

'They all have different policies, so of course they have to give different news.'

Evelyn Waugh, *Scoop*

The press is a flawed mirror into which thirty-two million Britons look every day. Its reflections, cracks, distortions, gaps and fragility have caused Parliament to send three Royal Commissions behind the looking-glass in three decades. The commissioners tend to report back from the Fleet Street wonderland that the mirror is the fairest of them all. Britain's press is free of government control, it is professional, its news columns are reasonably free of explicit bias, it has high standards of truth, it is aware of the need for ethical standards and has created a Press Council to remind it of them, it is not slavishly tied to party, it is interesting, it has popular papers which are popular and quality papers of quality, it is as free as can be expected of the direct influence of advertisers and proprietors. Yet it remains, in a fundamental sense, an unrepresentative press.

Newspapers are commercial products. They have to sell, and they have to sell advertising space. They thereby face a variety of commercial pressures. To some extent these are healthy. They encourage editors and journalists to write for readers rather than for themselves. Less effectively, they encourage newspaper managements to watch their costs and improve their efficiency. Some pressures are malignant. However, the evolution of the press in Britain in the eighty years or so since it became big business has been towards higher standards and towards an arm's length relationship between the editorial and business sides of a newspaper. A newspaper that did nothing but fawn on its readers or advertisers would not survive – but neither would a newspaper that disregarded the interests of its readers and the needs of its advertisers.

It is too readily assumed that newspapers have a commercial incentive to reflect the views and interests of people at large. They buy newspapers – therefore their views and interests are represented. Yes and no. It depends on how profitable it is – and is not – to represent them. Minorities with high spending power find themselves excellently catered for. Minorities who have less pull on advertisers find themselves neglected. There is no newspaper their money can buy. The imbalance in the representativeness of Britain's press resides not in what is, but in what is not.

Commercial pressures on the press have caused the closure of major national newspapers, have threatened to engulf others, and have deterred the creation of new newspapers. This is widely accepted as a matter of concern for democracy, and the demise of the production in Glasgow of the *Scottish Daily Express*, at the cost of 1 800 jobs, was one of the contributory factors in the setting up of the 1974 Royal Commission.

The long-diagnosed problems of the national press – over-manning, and declining circulations (which we shall see later is not such a problem) – had been joined by others. Newsprint prices doubled between 1972 and 1974, but newspaper cover prices were strictly controlled by the Prices Commission. As the economy deteriorated, the growth in advertising stopped and then began to fall. Costs continued to rise. Serious though these problems were, other more long-term commercial pressures on the democratic service provided by the press got much less attention than they deserve.

It is not enough that the decline in the number of national

newspapers has been partially filled by less cumbersome media in the shape of minority magazines and papers like *New Society*, *Private Eye*, *Socialist Worker* and the flowers of the press that bloom from underground (and just as suddenly wilt). Their influence on mainstream public and political opinion is at most indirect, filtering through national papers and the established weeklies. These continue to hold the attention of politicians, civil servants and businessmen. Fleet Street and its inner suburbs have also kept their grip on newspaper and television journalists themselves in identifying what is news and what makes an issue.

The mainstream British press has become increasingly polarized between what have become known as the popular papers at one pole, and quality newspapers at the other, the magnetic pole. Commercial success and survival depend on a newspaper getting its bearings right. The maps are drawn up with the help of advertisers and their market research analysts who patronize the newspapers that can deliver the right audience at the lowest cost. This has given rise to intensive research into who the readers are, and what they do – their social class, income and spending habits. Such categorization has played a growing part in determining the shape of the British press.

The research is extremely sophisticated. Advertisers can find out which publication has the most readers who are owners of colour televisions, or the most readers who are working wives with children, or who are middle-class car owners living in the north east. By combining this data with the advertising rates, advertising agents can work out for their clients which media offers the desired segment of the market at the cheapest rates. This is the most important factor, though not the only one, which guides advertising agents in their choice of which publications to use for their campaigns. Clearly specialist publications attract a particular segment of readership, and the advertising aimed at that market, and so do local publications. With national newspapers the segmentation that matters most is by social class.

The system of social grading now in common use for readership surveys was developed by the Joint Industry Committee for National Readership Surveys (JICNARS),[1] owned by those who need to know which spenders read what publication: the proprietors of national newspapers, magazines and periodicals, advertisers and advertising agents. Since the occupation of the chief earner largely determines the spending pattern of the household, social class is regarded as largely determined by jobs. There are six social grades.

The A households, the upper middle class, make up $2\frac{1}{2}$ per cent of all households. The head of the household is typically a successful business or professional man or senior civil servant who lives in a large detached house or expensive flat: people like surgeons, headmasters (of schools with over 750 pupils), executives near board level in companies with over 200 employees, chief officers in local government, chartered accountants, senior journalists and Church of England dignitaries (bishops or above). The Bs are the middle class and their households constitute 11 per cent of the total. They are quite senior people but not at the top of their profession or business, quite well-off but whose style of life is 'respectable rather than rich or luxurious'. Such as vicars, headmasters of smaller schools, senior executive officers in the civil service, university lecturers, matrons of smaller hospitals, pharmacists, small-company directors, and qualified librarians in charge of smaller libraries.

The C1 families, the lower middle class, are 23 per cent of the total, the small trades-people and non-manual workers, the 'white-collar' workers such as articled clerks, owners of small businesses, clerks, typists and telephonists, curates and nurses. Many of them earn less than those among the 33 per cent of C2 families classified as skilled working class – like foremen, fitters, knitters, plumbers, shop assistants with responsibilities, pastry-cooks and prison officers. The Ds are entirely manual workers either semi-skilled or unskilled; their families are 22 per cent of the total. Their jobs would, for example, be as labourers, fishermen, bus conductors, traffic wardens and window cleaners. The Es are the households at the 'lowest level of subsistence', and $9\frac{1}{2}$ per cent of households fall into that depressing classification.

They are the families of old age pensioners, widows and those dependent on social security.

Of the population at large, $13\frac{1}{2}$ per cent are As and Bs. The four quality dailies, the *Financial Times*, *The Times*, *The Daily Telegraph* and *The Guardian*, together draw an average of about 45 per cent of their readership from the ABs. For the quality Sundays, *The Sunday Times*, the *Sunday Telegraph* and *The Observer*, the combined readership profile shows that 39 per cent are ABs. This affluent readership attracts the advertising that permits quality newspapers to support themselves on relatively small circulations. It is these papers with a small but affluent readership base that are the ones read by decision makers in government and industry. Top civil servants questioned in 1967 for the Fulton Committee on the civil service were astute readers of *The Times*, *Guardian*, *Telegraph* and *Financial Times*, and of *The Sunday Times* and *The Observer* (though not the *Sunday Telegraph* – they preferred the *Sunday Express*) and of *The Economist*. Only 2 per cent regularly saw Britain's largest circulation newspaper, the *Daily Mirror*, and only 6 per cent saw the *Daily Express*.[2]

It is the quality newspapers that provide informed discussion of public issues, political affairs, business, the arts – of everything. They attract journalists of high skill and intellectual integrity. These papers provide a service indispensable for a liberal democracy in their news reporting and editorial analysis. The limitation – and it is less a limitation of the individual newspapers themselves than of the set of papers that exists – lies in the restricted nature of the service. They are obliged whether they like it or not (and many like it) to attract a readership with a high proportion of As and Bs, especially those As and Bs who either have high spending power or who, because of their positions in corporations or government, have influence over spending power. This distorts the overall balance of the press by giving the affluent readers an especially powerful voice through the press.

The quality papers have in recent years opened their pages to the expression of a wide range of political views. They have

Readership by social grade

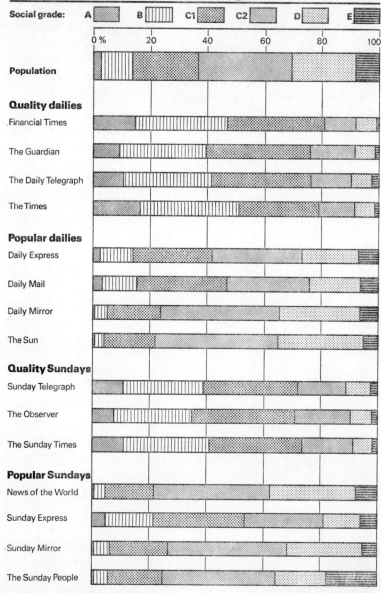

Social grade: A | B | C1 | C2 | D | E

0 %   20   40   60   80   100

Population

Quality dailies
Financial Times
The Guardian
The Daily Telegraph
The Times

Popular dailies
Daily Express
Daily Mail
Daily Mirror
The Sun

Quality Sundays
Sunday Telegraph
The Observer
The Sunday Times

Popular Sundays
News of the World
Sunday Express
Sunday Mirror
The Sunday People

Source: J I C N A R S National Readership Survey July 1973–June 1974.

published features and articles covering the political spectrum, some of them contributed by outsiders and including the unabashed left. Their own staff – especially their younger staff – have a somewhat greater opportunity than their predecessors to demonstrate political views diverging, usually to the left, from their paper's editorial line. A conscious attempt is made to avoid unfair reporting, especially as between the political parties. In a word, explicit bias is remarkably absent.

This does not make these papers a neutral influence on public affairs: papers attempting that would end up neutered. Indeed, they have not hesitated to reflect their current concerns and opinions in the selection and presentation of news. A good example was the treatment in *The Times* of 6 September 1974 of a speech by Sir Keith Joseph on inflation and unemployment which closely echoed the paper's editorial line of the time. The speech was printed verbatim in a prominent position in a type size larger than a report of a dull speech by the prime minister on the same day, a summary of the Joseph speech was the paper's front page lead and the treatment was rounded up in a sympathetic appraisal in a long first leader. Such practice would be criticized as an unjustifiable intrusion of editorial opinion into news reporting by the better American newspapers, with their somewhat formal distinction between fact and interpretation. But the old Printing House Square tradition of *The Times* as 'The Thunderer' is that a serious newspaper can be, and should be, a campaigning newspaper. That tradition prevents an undue concentration of news coverage of the men currently occupying positions of power. We therefore regard it as a healthy tradition in itself. The thing to do is to spread the campaigning around, not to suppress it.

Grounded on a small section of the community, which provides their livelihood, the quality papers' centre of gravity lies in the middle class and in the upper echelons of organizations. The issues they campaign on are naturally geared to this readership. Each paper serves its readers, but the upmarket bias leads to a social and ideological imbalance in the press as a whole, and to an undue conformity. This conformity becomes self-reinforcing since it influences the choice of senior editorial writers, and the criteria by which they in turn select news and treat stories.

Conformity spreads into radio and television. This is partly because journalists who write about things are asked to go to the studios and talk about them, but also because what they write itself makes a strong impression on programme planners and producers in broadcasting, who are apologetically conscious of the lack of a journalistic tradition of their own. A further influence in the same direction is the doctrine of impartiality, which encourages broadcasting executives to take positions behind the front lines and headlines established in the press.

On a number of major issues of the recent past, a common front taken up by the quality press, and extended to the popular press and broadcasting, has been far removed from the supposed ideal of diversity in the press. At the formative stages of the policy, the quality press had spoken almost with one voice, only to find qualifications and weaknesses in the consensus late in the day.

British entry into the common market is the most glaring example of this. The whole press, with the exception of the Beaverbrook newspapers which hankered after the ghost of Empire Free Trade, was in favour of entry. Without a committed anti-market quality paper, respectable and serious objections to the common market were limited to private discussions, academic seminars, Whitehall committee rooms and the activities of a few pamphleteers. So for all the millions of words it attracted, the issue was not given a full public airing. This one-sidedness and lack of debate evidently did little to persuade the British public, whose scepticism increased with the crescendo of press propaganda. But it probably did affect British decision-makers, in industry as well as government, and thereby contributed to a widening gap between rulers and ruled.

A second example illustrates a common neglect, rather than a common line: the neglect throughout the 1950s and 1960s of the question of the distribution of income and wealth. As Chapter 5 illustrates, discussion of the budgets and of fiscal policy was largely in terms of the management of demand in the economy and of the much-abused concept of economic growth.

A third example was the press consensus over the necessity for the industrial relations legislation of the Heath government to contain legal teeth (*The Guardian* was outside the consensus on this one). But once the teeth sank into the sensitive body of class and group loyalties and could not be unclenched without legal subterfuges, the press consensus switched almost overnight. It was then seen to be a bad idea to bring the law into industrial relations, which is what a good many managers and shop stewards had been saying all along. They were heard, but after the damage was done.

A fourth example was over the exploitation of North Sea oil and gas. When concessions were being negotiated, the government was told not to drive too hard a bargain. Five years later, there was righteous retrospective indignation when the softness of the terms was exposed by witnesses to a Parliamentary committee.

Conformity is a relative term. The consensus is a broad band, not a party line – not even a Fleet line. The picture that we suggest of the quality press is of a band of opinion and approaches occupying the broad centre of British politics from about half way into the moderate left through to the edges of the extreme right; with the individual papers occupying different and sometimes shifting positions within the band, and the band itself moving over time in response to events and political changes. But the most important characteristic of the consensus band lies not in the nuances of attitude taken on different items on the political agenda, but rather in the common agreement on that agenda itself – on the issues for discussion and the way in which they should be approached.

The preservation of even the present range of opinion within the broad consensus band is far from guaranteed. *The Guardian*, which pushes the band further left than it would otherwise be, is kept afloat by a combination of cross-subsidization and a family trust administered by men with an exceptional dedication to the priority of editorial conviction over commercial con venience. But this dedication itself exposes the paper to the periodic risks of financial collapse, of death by editorial conviction. A serious paper a little further to the left – or even one that attempted to carry radicalism further into its City columns – would not have survived that far.

To readers not accustomed to this way of looking at things – and above all perhaps to Fleet Street professionals – the approach summarized above is likely to provoke a number of immediate objections. In what sense is it justified to describe the upmarket influence as upmarket bias? Through what channels is this bias supposed to operate? Can papers that deal with public issues in a serious and thorough way exist on anything other than an upmarket readership?

The first objection is that newspapers – the mirror of society – reflect things as they are. And as things are, people with more income, wealth and influence get more of the good things of life like cars, houses, jobs, schools – and newspapers.

To the extent that newspapers are simply regarded as a consumer good, this objection is unanswerable. We prefer to regard them as incorporating a constitutional service vital for democracy. It is a basic principle of democracy that political influence should not be weighted by purchasing power, at least not too heavily. It should not be utopian to ask that each reader prepared to buy the newspaper of his choice with his or her money should weigh the same in the financial scales of the newspaper management. This is no more than consumer sovereignty, or 'dollar democracy' applied to newspapers as such. Indeed, this is implicitly assumed to be the case in those 'Why penalize the newspapers the public wants to read?' arguments. Yet in practice the bigger spenders enjoy a kind of plural voting in their influence on newspapers. It is rather like the plural votes that until 1950 were allocated to people with university degrees or more than one residence; they too were regarded as merely reflecting the different situations of the people concerned.

The second objection is that the quality papers have editors of high professional standing, to a large degree independent of management and proprietors, who are far from being mere sounding boards for their readers. On important occasions, they have taken a stand they believed to be right despite its evident unpopularity with their readers. The anti-government position taken by *The Guardian* and *The Observer* over the Suez conflict in 1956 is a prominent example. Where then is that link between the kind of people the readers are, and what the paper writes and stands for?

The most immediate connexion is the effect on the editor, feature writers, columnists and the news editor of how readers react. Where a matter of high principle is involved this reaction may be resisted, as in the Suez example above; otherwise it is not likely to be. In the longer run, there is an additional, stronger, connexion: the management is likely to select an editor who it hopes will have a rapport with the readers it particularly wants to retain or attract; and this editor is likely to give top billing to journalists who have a similar rapport. Journalists based outside such limits have few other places to go. The choice they are faced with is not the simple one of compromising either their intellectual integrity or their income and security; it is between continuing to exert some influence as against being not merely purer and poorer, but professionally impotent into the bargain.

In the end if editors do not respond to the interests and concerns of the readers the paper needs for its commercial viability, and management does not replace recalcitrant journalists, then the newspaper itself is unlikely to survive. In the long run, the unresponsive paper is dead. *The Observer* has never quite recovered from its Suez setback; *The Guardian* nearly went under there and then.

A third objection is that we are saying little more than that the quality press is the quality press, likely to be read by the readers with more education who predominate in the better jobs. Why should we expect working-class readers to be attracted to the qualities unless the qualities become more like the populars – and would that not mean a loss of both quality and diversity?

But looked at the other side up, approaching half of the readership of the quality press is outside the AB professionals – even, surprisingly, of the *Financial Times*. This shows that there is a substantial market for serious newspapers among the lower middle class and working class. One symptom of the upmarket bias is that these readers are not sought after; they are un-attractive to newspaper managements. Such readers are also simply less visible to the editorial department. A survey of the influential specialist correspondents of national news media, themselves predominantly middle class, found that they typically under-estimated the proportion of manual workers in their audience by twenty percentage points.[3]

The Times in 1968, at the peak of a big promotion drive, found itself with three-fifths of its readers in the lowly C1, C2, D and E groups. The advertisers were quick to notice; the man in the singlet made way for the keen-minded executive as *The Times* reader on station hoardings; and most of the newcomers were quickly shed. Admittedly this suggests that the singlet readers can hardly have felt *The Times* to be quite right for them, any more than *The Times* really felt they were right for it. But if these additional readers had attracted rather than repelled the advertisers, would the editor and his colleagues not have found additional coverage and material to hold them? Would such material have had to be any more out of character than the women's pages that, against similar fears, were laid on to attract the readers the advertisers did value?

When at the 1973 Labour Party Conference at Blackpool Mr Denis Healey outlined proposals for increased public expendi-ture that would increase the burden on taxpayers earning not quite twice the national average, his proposals had a poor reception in the quality papers. The most common criticism was not that such a fiscal package was undesirable or unfair, but that it risked alienating the centre in British politics. This is almost certainly untrue in electoral terms: only about one-tenth of British adults would be on the losing end of a redistribution financed at the expense of taxpayers earning not quite twice the national average. What is true is that this one-tenth of British adults indeed reaches the centre of the readership of the quality newspapers. The judgement made by these papers involved an implicit identi-fication of that readership with the nation as a whole. The identification was probably unconscious, and the more significant for that. The chart on page 16 should hang over the desk of all leader writers and political correspondents to be automatically illuminated on every use of the national 'we'.

References

1 MONK, Donald, *Social Grading on the National Readership Survey*, JICNARS, 1973.
2 PICKERING, J. F., survey in *Civil Service Committee 1966–68*, vol. 3 (2), p. 51.
3 TUNSTALL, Jeremy, *Journalists at Work*, Constable, 1971, p. 253.

2 The political context

'The printed word has always been the chief lieutenant of discontent, and if the hope of better things cannot find a lodging in the press much of the leaven will have gone out of society.'

Geoffrey Crowther, in *The Economist 1843-1943, A Centenary Volume*.

Newspapers play a constitutional and political role in society; that is why the effect of commercial pressures on the press is not merely a matter for Fleet Street or the Consumers' Association. Democracy requires a full and representative expression of the views and interests of all classes of the community. The community cannot expect to get this constitutional service from newspapers by the operation of commercial influences alone. To survive the vicissitudes of the market place, newspapers are under pressure to exploit the most profitable segments of the market – and to neglect rather than attract the less affluent readership.

The market economics of the press is not the ultimate source of the problem: the bias the press transmits, it does not itself create. The uneven distribution of political influence stems from the uneven distribution of income, wealth and economic power, and newspapers reflect the imbalance. To some degree they counteract it by helping to expose the use of economic power to the public eye. Newspapers also create some counter-power of their own against entrenched interests. But the British press has failed to do enough to open up the area of discussion and the range of views expressed. A corrective is needed to strengthen both the press and its contribution to political democracy.

By 1974, the quality press was itself concerned about prospective threats to democracy. Some of the comment was of the democracy-can-survive-only-on-our-policies variety, but there was a real and justified undercurrent of concern, which commonly focused on a single issue: inflation. But inflation in our society can climb to danger levels only as a result of irreconcilable social tensions.

The tensions underlying the British inflation of 1974 resulted from a complex set of influences, and no two commentators are going to agree on what the precise balance between them was. The problem was brought to a boil by the international price inflation of 1973–74, culminating in the enormous jump in the cost of oil. But it had been simmering under domestic fires long before – and people with quite different remedies for cooling those fires agreed that the deep political, social and industrial divisions in Britain had helped to keep them stoked. The press itself was down there in the boiler room and exerted a neglected – though far from dominant – influence on those divisions. To see why and how, the background to the dramatic events in the British political scene since the 1960s has to be sketched in.

A common problem in western democracies, which by the mid-1970s had become almost a cliché, has been the opening of a dangerous gulf between leaders and led. The Labour Party, formed to represent the interests of the working class in Parliament and to bring working men to Westminster, became increasingly dominated in its higher ranks by middle-class professionals. On the left wing of the Labour party this tendency was linked to the fact that the positive achievements of the Labour government of 1964 to 1970 were confined to essentially liberal reforms. In this stance the government was supported and to some extent strait-jacketed by the quality press. The press faithfully reflected a consensus of predominantly middle-class centrist opinion and interests. Its advice and criticism was given force through its impact on business confidence, which that Labour government felt bound to accept as a primary constraint.

When the Labour government lost the 1970 election, it became evident that a wide gulf had opened up between Labour leaders and constituency activists, but more importantly between the leaders and the workers on the shop floor. The press and television commentators, focusing on the divergence between the Labour government's actions on the one hand and the presumed path of enlightenment and righteousness on the other, virtually ignored this sector of mass opinion, and thereby contributed to the widening of the gulf. The Conservative government of Edward Heath came in dedicated to vigorous self-help policies. Its early actions in preparing its industrial relations legislation, in cutting taxes on high incomes and in making social welfare benefits more selective, received widespread press support. The gulf between government policy and shopfloor opinion widened further, and the mutual suspicion and mistrust culminated in the first miners' strike in 1972. The consensus band of centrist opinion moved a little to the left. The quality press urged reconciliation.

But now a dynamic process was under way. Organized labour had tasted power. Its confidence from the demonstration of its strength led it to paint the Labour party with a face of socialism that the power brokers in the party had in the past been able to brand as electorally unacceptable. A reluctant leadership was forced in 1973 to commit itself to bring about 'a fundamental and irreversible shift in the balance of wealth and power in favour of working people and their families'. By the time the minority Labour government was elected in February 1974, the polity that had commanded assent in the broad centre of British politics, including the Labour right, was undermined.

The natural reflex reaction of the quality press to this threat to the country's social stability was to revert to its home perch, that of the responsible middle-class professional. Its readers felt threatened; its writers perhaps more so. The immediate issue

was inflation; underneath lay a numbing feeling of control
slipping away. The stated concern was for the national interest.
This was genuine – but one's perception of the national interest
is coloured by one's instinct for one's own self-interest. Senior
journalists are themselves comfortably in the upper middle class
and are among the very highly paid, and the constituency of the
quality press is predominantly middle class. Yet these writers
had to judge – with these readers as their jury – the pros and
cons for the nation as a whole of measures designed to give the
upper middle class less of a general head start on others in wealth,
power and influence. Of course, these were not the only factors
involved, and many middle-class people believed that any significant shift of economic power threatened their personal and
political liberties, and those of the whole country. Others,
obviously including some manual workers, feared the influence of
union power as such.

We are not concerned here with the merits of the issues, but
with the diagnosis of the constellation of forces behind them. An
essential ingredient of that diagnosis should have been reporting
of the attitudes and opinion on the factory floor. Yet with peri-
pheral exceptions and worthy articles in *New Society*, this was
the last object of serious enquiry and analysis. The quality press
reported the views and gloom of London dinner parties and of
the City. To assess a foreign exchange crisis, sort out an
administrative tangle or understand a parliamentary manoeuvre,
this may be the best source of information. In an extended
industrial confrontation it is not.

The British quality press, increasingly oriented in the previous
twenty years to finance and management, was now left stranded
by the incapacity of finance and management to keep control.
Small wonder that the *Socialist Worker* found a ready market.
It and similar revolutionary sheets provided political views from
the factory floor. Less violent and less apocalyptic political
analysis from the same viewpoint was not available in the
upmarket press.

Following a speech in which Roy Jenkins more or less made
clear the terms on which he could stay in the Labour party, a

perceptive letter to *The Times* pointed out that the crucial battle
for allegiance was elsewhere:

Our statesmen of the right and of the centre are simply failing to face
the fact that the class consciousness of the contemporary Labour
movement surpasses anything which has been experienced since the
decade 1910–20. Mr Heath missed the point and met with disaster.
When Mr Jenkins shows anxiety about the mood of sullen uncertainty
in the private sector while entirely neglecting to take any account of
this far more formidable 'mood' he diminishes respect for his own
historical sense and his own political judgment.
(Professor Royden Harrison, Warwick University, 30 July 1974)

The complaint could have been directed as appositely at the press,
for which Mr Jenkins and his circle has long been a prime source
of information on the Labour party. What you pick up on the
Inner Circle from Fleet Street via Mansion House to Notting
Hill does not gain in veracity and significance from having been
deposited by other passengers travelling the reverse route.

A hint of the new balance of forces could have been gleaned
from a recurring story in the excellent foreign news pages of
the *Financial Times*. This reported a growing feeling among Italian
businessmen and bankers in 1974 that their economy could be
revived only by getting the communists into the government.
This prospect, the anathema of Italian politics for a quarter of
a century, was unwelcome to the entrenched politicians. It was
nonetheless seen by some powerful businessmen as the one
remaining means of engaging the co-operation of those who
ultimately made factories work.

It was a strange time to be playing that favourite parlour game
on the Inner Circle of hiving the bothersome left and militant
industrial wing of the Labour party off to leave what in substance
and perhaps in name would be a Centre party. Rather than
drawing attention to the 'Italian' perils of having the organized
working class beyond the political pale, the British quality press
busily promoted such a regrouping. Its narrow constituency no
longer coincided with the base of economic influence and power.
Its vision became blinkered, and its information service correspondingly inadequate.

A clue to this process of creeping obsolescence can be found in the identity of the authority called on most frequently by the quality press on occasions of high political *gravitas* – Walter Bagehot, the towering Victorian critic who among many other accomplishments was the most famous editor of *The Economist*. Bagehot had foreseen it all: 'The deference of the old electors to their betters was the only way in which our old system could be maintained'. Bagehot warned that the workers enfranchised by the 1867 Reform Act might not restrict themselves to deciding 'an issue selected by the higher classes'. And: 'a political combination of the lower classes, as such and for their own objects, is an evil of the first magnitude'.[1] But to quote Bagehot for foresight of what was in store for his class is one thing: to look to him in 1974 for guidance is to ignore that the world has changed in much the way that Bagehot himself feared. 'Do you think the laws of God will be suspended in favour of England because you were born in it?', asked Shaw's Captain Shotover. The laws of political power are equally unlikely to be suspended in favour of the class that happened to achieve ascendancy in the early stages of industrial capitalism. Or, to bring the point home, in favour of the AB reader of the British quality press. That press has to avoid being mesmerized by the perspective and interests of its own prime customers.

What can we expect from a representative and free press in a political democracy? In the consensus view, a free press fulfilling its constitutional responsibilities must satisfy the following criteria:[2]

(1) Full political independence from the government in the expression of its views and in its factual reporting;

(2) a reasonable degree of commercial independence from the direct influence of pressure groups and advertisers; sufficient diversity in the ownership of papers so that any influence exerted by proprietors is reasonably balanced (with a premium on the non-interference of management on editorial matters);

(3) a fairly close balance within individual papers in news coverage of major political parties; and no excessive imbalance in the press as a whole in editorial support of them.

This list covers the key concerns that are usually expressed. Yet the above attributes are not sufficient to ensure that the press:

(4) reflects the diversity in the range of viewpoint and opinion in the community at large;

(5) gives representative coverage to the range of interests of all sections of the community.

These two further criteria should be considered as prerequisites for political democracy. If the press does not reflect the full range of viewpoints and interests, then balance in coverage and support of the major political parties will mean more for the egos of party leaders than for wider political choice. For the lack of balance with which the press identifies and deals with fundamental issues must then be expected to influence the content of the party programmes themselves. At the crucial divide in modern British politics – between left and right within the Labour party – the mainstream British press, and regular television commentators along with it, are all on the same side. If party manifestos were written by those who comment on them, they would be of a uniform shade of grey.

The first set of criteria for the press – political independence, commercial independence, balanced party coverage – may be termed the liberal prerequisites. They are necessary to provide safeguards for personal liberty, to ensure against the abuse of power by government or by particular private groups and to provide a solid base for the alternation of government and opposition. They assure the electorate of a choice of men; not necessarily of measures.

The additional set of criteria for the press – reflection of the full range of viewpoints and of interests of all sections of the community – are necessary for political democracy in a fuller sense, though not a more extensive one than is the common aspiration for modern western democracy: broad equality of political influence for all citizens.

The press has traditionally had a key place in the reformer's armoury: 'the chief lieutenant of discontent', in the haunting phrase from Crowther's radical period. But the press has also served on the ramparts of the status quo. Those whose positions

were threatened used to defend themselves by acquiring newspapers or bribing them. In modern society the mechanism works
more subtly. Newspapers have a special incentive to cater for the
people with the most purchasing power. Newspaper sympathy
thereby comes automatically to the existing holders of money-
power through the advertising connexion. This is likely to bias
newspapers towards particular interests. More generally, the
natural stance of the upmarket press is to take the existing
distribution of purchasing power as given, and to question the
legitimacy of the use of electoral power to bring about major
economic and political change.

The use of parliamentary power to change the existing balance
of economic power is of course the rationale of democratic
socialist movements. The feasibility of such a transformation has
often been questioned from the left, for example, by Harold
Laski in the 1930s. Those in possession of established wealth and
power, it was argued, would not surrender them at the behest of
the ballot box; rather than lose the parliamentary game they
would put a stop to it. This issue was reopened by the rule and
overthrow of Salvador Allende, the Marxist president of Chile,
in 1970–73. Allende secured the largest share, but not a majority,
of the popular vote, and in a basically open régime he coun-
tenanced, or was forced to put up with, direct action groups
operating outside the law. The issue was not clear cut; in such
cases it rarely is. But the readiness of papers such as *The Times*
to equate such lapses with the military holocaust that followed
strongly suggested that the main concern was as much with
Allende's redistributionist aim as with his methods.

The uneasy question remained whether the defence of the
established positions of the middle and upper classes – positions
that can be labelled privileges or deserts according to taste – can
justify the overthrow of constitutional democracy and perhaps
also, as happened in Chile, destruction of civil liberties of the
population at large. The stand taken by influential organs of
opinion on this matter is of obvious importance. The 'regrettable

but inevitable' verdict on Allende was worrying to many people in Britain, since it could with a little imagination be carried forward to a future worldly sigh from the same papers for an authoritarian overthrow of a left-wing government in London. In fact, by the second election of 1974, *The Times* was talking editorially of the necessity of changing the electoral system in order to prevent 'the Allende disaster'. But what was the nature of the disaster? To implement a socialist programme without a full mandate and by the use of illegal measures? Or to attempt such a programme at all? The distinction was mostly blurred; but the impression was left that the use of electoral power to achieve a fundamental shift in economic power was in itself illegitimate. This was the old Laski thesis: the parliamentary game could stage only friendly matches.

Must democracy be undermined by more public ownership and a greater redistribution of wealth? Can a preventive suspension of democracy be justified to forestall government actions that appear themselves to threaten democracy? For those of us to whom the answers are not self-evident, it is particularly important that the issues should be thoroughly discussed from the viewpoints of all the different interests involved. The discussion that has so far taken place has been top heavy. It has reflected the upmarket bias of the press.

The 1970s have seen a revival in the British press of the ancient conservative doctrine that state action should not be used to influence the shape of society, but should be content to referee the society that emerges spontaneously from existing institutions and rights, including, for example, the ownership of property.

This doctrine was once the weapon used by the conservative right to oppose the liberal programme of social reform. As the reform programme of the liberal middle class has been largely completed, not least by Labour governments, this class in turn has felt increasingly threatened by further change from below. In the time-honoured manner of those who have battered their way through the gates that previously excluded them, the middle classes and the professions have perceived the wisdom of their ex-opponents. Suddenly, the newly arrived see the old force of the venerable and powerful argument by which Edmund Burke opposed the pretensions of the French revolution: it is vain to seek reasoned grounds to justify the organization of society, and it is folly to try and manipulate a developing organism that is too complex to understand or control.

The reappearance of this doctrine in British politics in itself offers an example of the way in which the serious press can radiate influence by acting as a bridge between the worlds of thought and of action. In performing this classic function it takes into account the concerns of its readers, but it decides where the bridges should be built, and thus what new substance is to be injected into the political debate.

The philosophy of modern conservatism has been developed most thoroughly by Friedrich von Hayek, who was brought over from Vienna in the early 1930s by Lionel (now Lord) Robbins to do battle with the economics of Maynard Keynes at Cambridge and the socialism of Laski and R. H. Tawney at the London School of Economics. Hayek's inaugural lecture of 1933 set out the essence of his approach to which he has adhered ever since. Standing aside from intellectual fashion in true scholastic form, he eventually saw fashion change and embrace him, with the 1974 Nobel prize as his public recognition. The key elements in Hayek's writings were republished in pamphlet form in 1972 by the Institute of Economic Affairs, which has made itself the most effective of Britain's pro-capitalist boosters by its appreciation that serious, if selective, research work makes far better propaganda than slogans.

For Hayek, a largely unregulated market economy is an indispensable safeguard of personal liberty. Thus Hayek had opposed the pragmatic element in Keynesian interventionism, which formed the basis of the postwar consensus both in economic policy and in the managerial, non-ideological approach to politics. By the early 1970s, Keynesian management by itself was clearly seen to be inadequate from whatever political standpoint it was viewed. A great big hole appeared where the centre had been.

Hayek's openly ideological assault on government intervention in pursuit of piecemeal social improvement[3] found a new audience. In particular it struck a chord with Britain's most influential economic journalist of the time, Samuel Brittan of the *Financial Times*;[4] he in turn had a decisive influence on Peter Jay, the economics editor of *The Times*, also the presenter of what was probably the most sophisticated current affairs programme on British television. The editor of *The Times*, William Rees-Mogg, had himself added an economic dimension to the traditional responsibility felt by his office for national salvation, and the approaches gelled. Through the medium of Sir Keith Joseph, this new-old economic philosophy was injected into the centre of British politics in the autumn 1974 election campaign.

Hayek also proposed limiting the legislative powers of the elected parliament by subordinating it in key respects to a new chamber of elders. This interpretation of the limited scope for legislative change in a democracy was a stronger version of another attempt to curtail the extent of change by emphasizing the pluralist nature of the democratic state. There are in this view various centres of power in a democracy – such as business, the wealthy, trade unions, the City, etc. – and they function alongside as well as through the elected government. They act as countervailing restraints not only against each other but also against the abuse of state power itself. The lobby and the pressure group are seen not just as admissible influences but as necessary components of pluralist democracy. Each social and economic group has, in effect, a veto power on change, a defensive right that the electoral mandate does not override.

This interpretation of the concept of pluralism gained strength and respectability in the United States in the 1950s and became the orthodoxy of American political science; it gained indirect support from what may seem a surprising source. The book that introduced John Kenneth Galbraith to the general public was *American Capitalism: the Concept of Countervailing Power*. Economic power in the modern capitalist society, as seen by this prominent critic on the liberal left, was nothing more than a stand off: big business had to contend with big labour, big sellers

B

with big buyers. In Britain, the most influential work on democratic socialism in the post-war generation, Anthony Crosland's *The Future of Socialism*, also took an essentially benign view of the existing concentrations of economic power.

The exercise by the trade unions of something like their full bargaining strength has upset the rather cosy picture of strong groups battling each other into stability. When a substantial proportion of the population does get organized, and each group seeks to use its organized power to maximize its collective gain, the result is disruptive and wasteful, and is now widely seen as such. The most important source of such waste and disruption in Britain has been the aggressive and competitive wage bargaining by the trade unions. However, the press picture of trade union leaders as industrial barons beyond the rule of the law is incomplete. There are other important barons, sometimes disguised as gnomes, who influence state action outside the ballot box; they are treated as part of the scenery. It is taken for granted that governments should respond to industrialists making their views felt in speeches and through their investment decisions, or to financial interests speaking through the performance of the stock market, or to bankers because of the state of foreign confidence in sterling or to a whole set of interest groups through their social and professional contacts with ministers and officials.

From the perch of the press, these extra-parliamentary constraints are part of the facts of life in which governments, especially Labour governments, have to work. But when the pressure is exerted by trade unions, it becomes a threat to democracy rather than a part of it. Some pressure groups are woven so closely into the fabric that they become invisible. Or perhaps it is that all pressure groups are invisible to those within them.

The press likes to see itself as an agent for change, reforming and crusading. On a myriad of matters, exposure in the press has put a stop to a piece of bureaucratic inanity, government stupidity or selfish chicanery. Fleet Street editors love to see themselves as people who help to right many wrongs. They do, but in a deeper sense the press can be seen as something else – as part of the resistance-to-change movement.

The influence of the press on particular events including general elections is notoriously limited.[5] Much more important is the broad influence over the climate of opinion, an influence which sets the boundaries and to a large extent the agenda of political action, which in turn helps determine the content of party programmes. The most important question in politics is not who wins the conflict, but what the conflict is about; not what the decision is, but if there is to be one, or whether a non-decision will simply flow automatically from a climate of opinion formed by an initial compromise.[6]

For years, discussion of the British balance of payments raged with the most important element in the problem – abandonment of an overvalued exchange rate – *hors de combat*. For years, discussion of incomes policy remained confined to technique, divorced from the wider questions of income distribution. Then, as a result of new pressures, these hidden issues leaped to the agenda. Therefore, to determine where power and influence reside, one has to look at public decisions in the light not only of the stated alternatives, but also of those excluded because they seemed obviously unacceptable. The real power is exercised in keeping items off the agenda, as every crafty bureaucrat – and parent – knows.

The press has an important influence on the agenda. It alone is the judge of that elusive concept: news value. Those who dominate the selection process are a small group of editors, news editors and columnists. They make the best judgement they can of what interests and concerns their readers. In this judgement, the press is inevitably influenced not only by what it knows about its readers, from their social class to their hobbies, but also by the ambience in which journalists, and particularly editors and news editors, themselves move, both professionally and socially. This latter influence is often suspected of reinforcing the middle-class and London-centred focus of the press.

What the press does not write about or campaign about is certainly as important as its positive contribution, where it often simply reflects other forces in society. As an academic analyst has put it: 'Broadly speaking, newspapers determine what we think *about* more than what we think'.[7] So the question of which forces of society the press does not reflect, or reflects weakly, is crucial. 'The influence of the press is in the steady plugging way of affecting the subconscious, semiconscious and subliminal and not on specific bills before Parliament or on elections.' So Geoffrey Crowther told the Shawcross Commission in 1961, from many years' experience of the most skilful plugging in his paper, *The Economist*. Academic studies confirm the view that the media tend to have a negligible impact on attitudes on specific issues in the short term; they tend to reinforce opinions rather than convert them. But the long term impact of the press is another matter. Determining what we think about is quite important.

References

1 *The English Constitution*, Introduction to the Second Edition.
2 Drawn *inter alia* from the 1947 Royal Commission on the Press (Cmd. 7700), from extensive evidence to the 1961–62 Shawcross Commission (Cmd. 1811). See also: WINTOUR, Charles, *Pressures on the Press*, André Deutsch, 1972, and KLEIN, Rudolf, Political Quarterly 1973, pages 33–46.
3 HAYEK, F. A., *Law, Legislation and Liberty*, his latest presentation being published in three volumes by Routledge and Kegan Paul. See also his *Economic Freedom and Representative Government*, Institute of Economic Affairs, 1973.
4 BRITTAN, Samuel, *Capitalism and the Permissive Society*, Macmillan, 1973, and *Economic Contradictions of Democracy*, British *Journal of Political Science*, April 1975.
5 McQUAIL, Denis, *Towards a Sociology of Mass Communication*, 1969, Collier-Macmillan, pp. 45–46; SEYMOUR-URE, Colin, *Political Impact of Mass Media*, Constable, 1974, Chap. 2.
6 'Compromise . . . enters into the initial determination of the limits of controversy: only a small band of the full range of alternative policies is effectively ventilated and disputed. Indeed, on some issues the band may be so narrow that decisions seem not to be "made" at all – they just flow automatically from the "climate of opinion" formed by the initial compromise.' WESTERGAARD, J. H., 'Sociology: the Myth of Classlessness', *Ideology in Social Science*, ed. Robin Blackburn, Fontana/Collins, 1972, p. 140.
7 SEYMOUR-URE, Colin, 'Editorial Policy Making', *Government and Opposition*, Autumn, 1969, page 428.

3 The upmarket press

We do not believe, for example, that the 206 000 people in business earning less than £3 000 can be viewed as being of much importance.

Media Planning Study prepared by the *Financial Times*, 1973.

The last chapter discussed the various ways – subtle, indirect and long term – by which the press exerts influence on public affairs. This chapter is concerned with the commercial factors that help shape that influence as a resultant of the peculiar economics of the newspaper business.

In the past, the influence exerted by the press appeared to have an obvious source. It was associated, both in Britain and the United States, with the views of the newspaper proprietors. They had no compunction in using their newspapers as a vehicle for the expression of their views, along with making money from them. Among these pioneer press lords, the only variation lay in which of these two objectives, making money and making propaganda, was the primary one. But the press lords of the present generation have shown a general change of emphasis and style. These tycoons in business accountancy are less interested in what their papers say than in what they pay. As Lord Thomson put it to the Shawcross Commission with his engaging directness: 'You just cannot have common editorial views. For instance, in the textile areas of this country they are all for protection of textiles . . . in Wales and in Cardiff they could not care less.'

This change in the character of newspaper proprietorship has been widely noted almost always with approval. Harold Wilson has been among the most hearty applauders – at least of this aspect of the newspaper industry. But the potential benefits of the switch have been exaggerated, and the limitations barely noticed. There have been certain obviously beneficial results, notably in removing an arbitrary force for the pursuit of personal vendettas, both in editorial policy and in staff appointments. But the switch to accountant control has not improved the representativeness of the 'steady plugging' influence of the press, nor can it be expected to do so without further changes. This is because the underlying source of this influence resided not so much in the proprietorial whims exercised in colourful but sometimes ominous ways, as in the internal economics of the newspaper business.

Newspapers are among the few products for which one buyer's money is not as good as another's in the eyes of the seller: 8p a day from a reader earning £5000 a year is worth much more than 8p from a reader earning £2000 a year, because a newspaper is not just selling its editorial product to its readers but is selling its readers' incomes to advertisers. There is an underlying pressure on newspaper managements, whether run by cranky individualists or straight-laced accountants, to do one of two things: to upgrade the readership, and thereby deliver a higher aggregate of readers' incomes without an offsetting increase in costs, which means getting a high proportion of AB readers; or to go for low costs and mass readership, so that what the readers lack in commercial quality they make up for with quantity – of their aggregate incomes for the advertisers, and of their daily pennies for the newspaper. Once the initial strategy has been set, the room for manoeuvre is small.

The advertising connexion has operated in recent years in a way that tends to increase the polarization of newspapers. This has not always been so. Before the advent of commercial television, newspapers such as the *Daily Express* and *Sunday Express* which had readerships covering a wide range of social groups were sought after by advertisers selling in the mass market.

Now advertisers who seek blanket coverage of the mass market can get this more effectively from television. Newspapers tend to be used largely to supplement television and fill in what it misses – the specialist markets and the light television viewers. This development partly explains the improved position of some quality papers and the decline in the fortunes of newspapers appealing to a wide range of social groups, like the *Daily Express* and the *Daily Mail*. Safety today lies in the appeal to a cohesive socio-economic group, the more well-heeled the better. As Charles Wintour, the editor of the *Evening Standard* has said, 'The advertiser wants a coherent group of readers, not a wide scatter';[1] this influences the basic strategy of a newspaper.

The peculiar economics of the press have three main characteristics. First, newspapers are a very special case of 'joint supply'. The textbook example is the sheep, whose body satisfies the meat market and whose coat supplies the wool market. Since the cost of rearing the beast has to be recouped in both markets, the breeder has to watch the price of wool and of lamb chops. But at least the demand for wool and that for lamb chops are independent. Not so with newspapers. The two demands that a single newspaper has to meet are the demands of the reader for a good and satisfying product and of the advertiser for a readership that he wants to reach. But the one depends very much on the other. The advertiser buys advertising space, but the value to him of that space depends on the number of readers who see it, and on the purchasing power at their command. Newspapers have to do a juggling act, described in more detail in Chapter 4, to get the two sources of revenue, circulation and advertising – both of which have repercussions on costs – into the right relationship with each other.

Second, high overheads are unavoidable for the production of newspapers. Before the first copy can be printed, a newspaper has to have its plant, offices, staff and distribution network. Then, with each successive copy, the cost per copy falls dramatically until very high circulations are reached. In technical economic terms, newspaper production enjoys increasing returns to scale. A newspaper with a large circulation has lower unit costs than newspapers with smaller ones, and can undercut them in price. The amalgamation of two unprofitable newspapers can lead to the emergence of a single, strong and profitable one – as has happened to local newspapers in nearly every city and town in Britain. This reflects in part the usual gains of monopoly as well as the economies of scale. But high overhead costs give a built-in incentive to cut-throat competition.

Third, the cost advantage of the big battalions is compounded by the advertising advantage. As sales go up, not only are average unit costs reduced by the spreading of overheads referred to above, but also the newspaper can charge a higher rate to advertisers who can reach more readers with each insert, at little extra cost to itself.

So advertisers are not interested in readers as such, but in readers who buy their products, or absorb their image. The attraction of a given paper to the advertisers will therefore depend on the combination of two elements: the number of readers and their ability to buy or absorb. The average reader of the *Daily Mirror* may buy more HP Sauce than the average reader of the *Financial Times*, and the average reader of *Photography* more cameras. But the predominant influence on spending is income: the rich buy more of most things than the poor. It is the quality of their readers' incomes that enables the quality newspapers, whose circulations are too small to benefit much from production economies, to pay their way.

Better-off readers have more money for their own spending. As fashion leaders they may start a spending trend. More important, their professional or business positions often give them influence over corporate spending so that much advertising is directed to the business reader as businessman, rather than consumer. Advertising of this kind has shown by far the greatest expansion in recent years and gave birth to a litter of business sections and supplements, and the chase after the executive reader. The same influence might explain the remarkable upward mobility enjoyed by financial journalists in Fleet Street in recent years. *Punch*, the weekly comic of the middle class, blossomed as an advertising medium when a financial journalist, William

Davis, became editor. The editors of *The Times*, the *Financial Times* and *The Daily Telegraph* in late 1974 had all started as financial journalists; the editor of the *Daily Express*, Alastair Burnet, had been plucked from *The Economist* in what looked like a bankers' bid to go upmarket with a professional in that business. We pointed out in the last chapter that an important medium range influence on the press lay in the kind of people who were selected as editors. The new vogue in favour of financial journalists seems to be an example of that influence. They have the capability and inclination to steer their papers in the direction the management wants to go, and perhaps must go if it is to stay afloat. The editors have full editorial freedom, but they are also expected to bring home the bacon.

The importance to a newspaper's management of the income and spending power commanded by its readers is best summarized by a single statistic: the willingness of advertisers to pay over six times more to reach a given number of readers of the *Financial Times* than the same number of readers of the *Daily Mirror* (table 3.1). As the *Daily Mirror* has fifteen times the readership of the *Financial Times*, the actual cost per column-inch is two and three-quarters times higher in the *Mirror*. Both these papers are profitable; their contrasting situations are a graphic illustration of how the number of readers needed for the commercial viability of a newspaper varies directly with the income and social class of the readers. About 900 000 readers (some 200 000 buyers: each copy of a newspaper is read by between two and a half and four and a half people) bring high prosperity to the *Financial Times*, with the best economic reporters, political commentators and foreign correspondents that money can buy; five times that many readers were deficient for the pre-Murdoch *Sun*.

Yet the dual standard that determines the number of readers needed for commercial viability is so deeply embedded into Fleet Street's subconscious that it is ignored. So we are told that the *Herald*, the pre-Murdoch *Sun* or the *News Chronicle* failed because they did not get enough readers, rather than that their readers were insufficiently attractive to advertisers. The same number of top people taking *The Times* would be celebrated

Table 3.1 The millinch test

	Circulation 000s	Readership 000s	Readership profile %			Rate per column inch £	Millinch rate p	Advertising as % of total revenue
			A	B	C_1			
Financial Times	199	900	15	32	34	17·00	2·12	80
The Times	351	1 200	16	34	28	17·80	1·62	73
The Guardian	365	1 200	9	31	36	16·00	1·45	57[E]
The Daily Telegraph	1 427	3 600	11	31	35	29·00	0·82	60[E]
Daily Mail	1 768	5 100	3	13	31	25·50	0·49	42[E]
Daily Express	3 227	9 200	3	12	28	37·00	0·40	39[E]
Daily Mirror	4 192	13 500	1	4	19	46·75	0·34	31
The Sun	3 303	11 400	1	4	18	35·00	0·33	26[E]

Circulation, January–June 1974, Audit Bureau of Circulation; Readership, July 1973–June 1974 JICNARS National Readership Survey; Advertising rates, British Rates and Data; Advertising proportion, which includes both display and classified, obtained from newspapers or (E) estimated for 1973; Millinch rate is the advertising rate per column inch per 1 000 readers.

as an editorial jackpot. Readers are weighed, rather than counted. That is the Fleet Street market bias.

The wooing of top people and of the business reader by the press has a number of important effects on the character of the press – on newspapers that are successful, on those that are not, and in explaining the non-existence of papers that might otherwise exist. They are discussed under eight headings.

1. Aiming for the centre

When a small number of firms compete, there is a tendency for all of them to aim at the centre and for their products to be different only in the incidentals. The classic illustration of this tendency has been the American motor industry, which, with a huge market and a wide range of different tastes, found it most profitable to produce a range of cars remarkable only in their similarity; buyers who wanted something as eccentric as a small car or a sports car had to turn to imports. The increasing conformity of the British quality press, in style and in substance, is an example of this fundamental tendency of oligopolistic competition to serve the centre of the market at the expense of minority tastes.

The best way of visualizing this tendency is a strip of road in the desert evenly populated from mile 0 where the road begins, to mile 100 where it ends. If there are only two petrol stations, the placing that will give best service to consumers will be at miles 25 and 75. This would be the placing selected by a private or public monopoly as long as it maintained two stations. Competition will drive both stations towards the centre, eating into each others' market, the increasingly isolated customers at both extremes having nowhere else to go. This phenomenon has been discussed in the economic literature in the context of television, but has not been applied to newspapers.[2]

But in newspapers there is an additional kink: the market is for newspapers plus the products and images advertised in them, so that the centre of the market in terms of newspaper revenue is not the centre of the market in terms of newspaper readers.

Another example of competition among a few large firms leading to conformity is commercial television and radio in the United States – though in the case of radio, those areas large enough to support many stations, such as New York and Los Angeles, do indeed provide variety with a real choice offered to minorities.

There is an interesting contrast in behaviour by conglomerate groups publishing both newspapers and books. Books are sold as books, not as the vehicles for the advertising of other products. Publishers have an incentive to produce the books they think the reading public will buy. Because buyers of paperbacks on political and economic subjects are inclined to the left, it has always been easier for an author writing to a general audience to find a publisher for a critique from the left than for a critique from the right or a defence of the status quo. When the S. Pearson conglomerate, which owns the *Financial Times*, acquired Penguin Books, this political slant was maintained, corresponding as it did to the slant of the potential readership. Episodes such as this are alternatively lamented as capitalism's suicidal self-destruction[3] or coolly celebrated as evidencing the political neutrality of the profit maximizing system.[4] But profit maximization cannot be expected to lead to a similar neutrality between the tastes of different buyers when the product on sale is not books, but the package of editorial and advertising that constitutes a newspaper. The profits of Pearson are unaffected by whether its Penguins are bought by the surtax or the student class; they are directly affected by which class of readers buys the *Financial Times*.

2. The band of acceptable opinions

The need to appeal to the business audience, or at least to a concentration of affluent readers, inevitably sets limits on the degree of radicalism or non-conformity in editorial policy. This influence need not imply any direct or explicit dictation of editorial policy by management. That will not usually be necessary. Influence works at a number of levels and through a number of links. It determines the kind of people who are selected as editors, the kind of leader writers and columnists who emerge, and finally, the papers that succeed and survive. Thus the relevant question to ask about what determines the influence of the press is less often 'Why does Editor X or Journalist Y have the views (or pliability) he has?' than 'Why does X or Y, with his views (or pliability), have the position he has?'

Significantly more Fleet Street journalists are to the left of their organizations than to the right.[5] They evidently lack outlets – or at least sufficiently lucrative outlets – with their own political slant. They are prepared to work within the acceptable inner band of the political spectrum, a band that extends a limited distance to the left and right of the consensus centre of the moment. Those journalists not prepared to work within such limits risk either staying on the sidelines (or worse) in their own organization; or, if they step outside the established press, they risk both the loss of an assured audience of key decision makers, and a drastic reduction in salary, security and fringe benefits.

Consider the distinctive style of British press and television journalism in the past decade – abrasive in manner, critical of the practitioners of power, unquestioning of the foundations of power. It is a style that nicely meets the latent demand for righteous indignation about the way other people behave, while at the same time indulging our wishful evasion of the question of what society can realistically do about it. It does not confront fundamental questions of choice. Such questions would destroy the glow of shared concern produced by exposure of the incompetent or the wicked and would have an unfortunate tendency to divide readers according to their political views. Just what a modern editor-in-chief seeks to avoid.

The asking of questions in a form that precludes serious answers achieves commercial success – but at a cost to the community. The style manages to sap the authority of the existing institutions without laying a basis for anything to take their place. This is a grievance that both political conservatives and political radicals can share against the mainstream British press and television.

In a penetrating analysis of *Private Eye*, Colin Seymour-Ure crystallizes the phenomenon as 'The Politics of the Fool'. ('The Fool loves the King because his security is linked to the King's security. Without the King as a butt, he has no role.')[6] In a wider critique of the British press as a whole, an influential Conservative MP, Douglas Hurd, pointed out that *Private Eye* had influenced the quality press in one dubious way: 'The press has become simultaneously more volatile and more like-minded. At any given moment most editors and most political correspondents will join in damning a government which perhaps six months earlier they were praising.'[7] Although a piece of special pleading, the complaint had an element of truth. The growing detachment of the press as a whole from particular parties and committed positions has its good side, but it has also meant some loss in intellectual responsibility. Fleet Street is full of snipers.

3. Word pollution

The pull of high incomes and business readership affects the character not only of the papers catering to that readership but also that of the press as a whole. The development of large, professional and glossy papers may leave readers dissatisfied with the thinner, greyer products they were once happy with. This makes it even more difficult for a newspaper to get off the ground; it has to look impressive from the first issue.

While the heavies and the glossies may redirect some people back to the unleavened black and white purity of treatment in publications like *The Times Literary Supplement* or the *New York Review of Books*, the richness of texture of the serious press does force the mind to accept the most strident incongruities. There is something unreal about a report on the stresses (STRESS! STRESS! STRESS!) of modern life in *The Sunday Times* Colour Magazine,[8] followed by sixteen pages of 'When you can't afford a £300 Sonata Suite, what are the alternatives? *Three-piece Sonata Suite £287.25 . . .', 'The 150 mph headlight, good news for some, no news for others', 'For the price of 153 visits to your local Safari park . . . we'll give you 15 days in East

Africa', and all the other eye-catching ways of spending money that people suffer stress earning.

The colour supplements provide the space and the resources for articles that would otherwise not get anywhere near a newspaper, but to some extent their setting detracts from their worth. There is an incongruity in surrounding an article on the hungry in Bangladesh with pictures of luxurious kitchens. There is a further, unfathomable point. The flood of commercially-inspired writing and messages may engender a suspicion of the written word in general. Among the billions of words manufactured daily in brochures, jargon-diseased reports and memoranda, party propaganda and everything else, the articles in the newspapers of western democracies and a few other countries belong to the precious minority of wordage that the reader feels he can more or less take on trust. It is easy to become cynical about newspapers (although one also has to guard against being unduly pious) and advertising supplements carrying a decorative surround of editorial matter may weaken the reader's trust in the urgency and honesty of what is in the press as a whole.

4. The exposé as binge

The big, financially secure newspaper groups claim that they use their resources to do team investigative reporting and to bear the subsequent legal costs of defending their stories. The most famous piece of team investigation, that by Bob Woodward and Carl Bernstein leading to the exposure of the Watergate affair, could have been done only by a large and secure newspaper like the *Washington Post*. In Britain, *The Sunday Times* Insight team has set new standards of in-depth (sometimes boring-to-depth) reporting, though hampered by Britain's strict laws of libel and contempt of court and by the Official Secrets Act. Huge teams are not the only way to get good stories, as I. F. Stone showed with his one-man Washington newssheet in the United States and Paul Foot showed in Britain with his 'Footnotes' in *Private Eye*. Perhaps there was less entertainment value and less minute-by-minute story-telling, but the impact was made.

There is a tendency for exposés to be of the post-mortem variety. The forthright and entertaining exposé of Investors Overseas Services and Bernard Cornfeld in *The Sunday Times* in 1971 mentioned in passing that a damning report on IOS was issued by the Dutch Consumers' Association five years earlier. Its resources must have been a minute fraction of those available to the British financial press. A number of City editors had their suspicions of Cornfeld while he was riding high, but kept quiet about them while their pages were being swollen by his advertisements.

Exposés of real worth are by no means unknown in the British press. The thalidomide campaign of *The Sunday Times* and *The Guardian*'s campaign on wages paid in South Africa by British firms are two prominent examples. Both these campaigns were within the limits of what the relevant consensus – intelligent opinion in the business establishment – found acceptable. The South African campaign could probably not have been run two years earlier, when it would have been too far 'ahead'. More significant still, there is a strict limit to the number of such campaigns that a newspaper can run without risking financial suicide. *The Guardian*'s South African campaign probably lost it advertising. Incisive exposés of this type have the character of the binge for the established press – occasional splashes that if indulged in too often will spell financial ruin.

5. The establishment embrace

It can be inhibiting for a newspaper to be an important business establishment. An example is provided by the long press silence on the subject of devaluation before 1967. By the summer of 1967 the then editor of the *Financial Times*, Sir Gordon Newton, had become convinced that devaluation was inevitable. But he continued to ban direct references to either its likelihood or its desirability, which he feared (probably on solid grounds) would tempt Harold Wilson to make the City of London in general and the *Financial Times* in particular a scapegoat for such an unpopular act. *The Economist*, which had convinced itself of the need for devaluation years earlier, adopted essentially the same self-censorship. So the views of these papers was made known only to their luncheon guests. In this important matter, the press reinforced the two-tier information system, of those in the know and the rest, rather than extending the available information – in this case the true views of these influential journals – to the public at large, which should be its job.

The cosy relationships in British public life are conducive to acts of self-censorship in the interests of the state, though the less noble desire to protect the position of the newspaper as a commercial concern is bound up with such acts. Official disapproval may cut off sources of information, of respect and friendship and eventually might also harm the business interests of the newspaper's owners. The larger the business, and the more established the position of the newspaper and its journalists in national life, the greater these combined pressures tend to be. The position of the quality press as part of the nation's establishment is a mixed blessing.

6. Our special correspondent with the workers (delayed)

A forgotten casualty of catering for an élite readership is the loss of information to the press itself. The quality press reflects middle-class concerns, including middle-class concerns about the working class. On the whole it failed to report the reception given to the industrial relations legislation, and the depth of the opposition on the shop floor. The problems of child poverty were brought to the attention of the press (and thereby of government) by a determined pressure group. The tax trap of the working poor was publicized in an 'exposé' by a research group which showed that the effective marginal tax rates could go over 100 per cent. The upmarket press, with its talk of the necessity for greater incentives, had its eyes riveted on the upper income groups; the press did not need Cambridge economists to tell it about their tax gripes. This information gap also leads to a kind of issue cycle, with themes leaping into general prominence only to be forgotten and buried with equal suddenness.

7. The imperialist impulse

If a paper's expansion into its AB market has reached a natural limit, further expansion beyond it represents the forbidden temptation subject to the terrible punishment of diluting the commercial quality of the readership. Commercial expansion is then limited to two directions: first, outside the newspaper business altogether, through diversification; second, through expansion abroad. It is still hard to sell a daily newspaper in another country because of the transport costs, the impossibility of getting newspapers into foreign hands before they are out of date, and language barriers. The weeklies have been able to build up a substantial readership abroad because they are not so tied to the news; *The Economist*'s sale has been split roughly equally between home and overseas since it began life in the mid-nineteenth century. But the growing number of international businessmen with homogeneous interests and similar lifestyles has opened up an opportunity for foreign expansion in the most profitable sector of the newspaper market. With English the language of international business and the skill of British newspapers at handling business journalism, the London quality press has an advantage in this competition, as the survey on what top Europeans read shows (table 3.2; *The Times*, which commissioned the survey, comes out particularly well).

The Times early on announced itself the newspaper of Europe; others followed suit. Its management recognized the possibility of collecting together a segment of European ABs, and got over the language and time barriers in an ingenious way. It joined with three other European top people's newspapers – *Le Monde*, *La Stampa* and *Die Welt* – to produce a monthly with the inevitable name of *Europa* which is slipped inside each of the four papers in its home language. The end result is not a bad product, but bears the marks of being a product deliberately manufactured to fill a marketing niche, without any soul of its own or real purpose. The *Financial Times* has also been trying to get itself on the bookstalls of Europe, if only to catch the eyes of European placers of advertising.

In soliciting readers and advertisers among European business-men both *The Times* and the *Financial Times* naturally stressed the editorial support they gave to British entry into the common

Table 3.2: What top Europeans read

Percentage of European businessmen and politicians reading indicated newspaper in 1971

Businessmen Occasional Readership		Businessmen, Politicians, and Civil Servants Regular Readership*	
The Times	81	Le Monde	37
Financial Times	78	The Times	36
The Daily Telegraph	53	Financial Times	28
Le Monde	52	Neue Zurcher Zeitung	21
International Herald Tribune	47	Le Figaro	18
Le Figaro	43	International Herald Tribune	18
Wall Street Journal	42	Frankfurter Allgemeine	17
Frankfurter Allgemeine	39	The Daily Telegraph	16
The Guardian	39	Die Welt	12
Neue Zurcher Zeitung	38	The Guardian	10

* 'On average at least 4 out of 6 issues'.

Based on a sample of politicians and businessmen in western Europe (EEC, EFTA and Spain) drawn from International Who's Who, conducted by Research Services Ltd. for *The Times*. Just under one quarter of the sample was of respondents in Britain.

Source: 'Europe Today', *The Times*, 1971.

market and subsequently to the formulation of European policies. Thus, advertisements placed by the *Financial Times* soliciting European readers and advertisers in 1971, began: 'The *Financial Times* has always been in favour of Britain joining the European

Economic Community.' It was taken for granted that there was a connexion between editorial view and business strategy. The top management of the *Financial Times* arranged a series of receptions in business centres of the EEC, with a member of the staff in attendance to explain the paper's editorial policy. Our implication is not that those responsible for editorial opinion have been pressured by management exigencies: they include some enthusiastic advocates of European federalism. The implication is that any journalist with strong reservations about the European venture and a determination to express them, would not, once the management course was set, have been moved into a central place in these papers' editorial policies.

Much puzzlement has been expressed about the near unanimity of the British press in favour of the common market even though public opinion at large was hostile, as were many people in the universities and the civil service. The unrepresentative stance taken by the press on this issue has a number of explanations, including the remarkably effective lobbying and infiltration achieved by the 'pro-EEC faction'.[9] But surely the interests of the newspaper business as such were important. Newspapers that saw their own prosperity bound up with common market entry doubtless found it easier to believe the same was true for everyone else.

The newspapers that dominate the reporting and discussion of British economic and political policy are widening their constituency beyond the national frontier to the international executive class. A casual impression of the extent to which this tendency has gone can be gained by flipping through the pages of the *Financial Times* or *The Economist* and noting the proportion of foreign or multinational corporations among the advertisers. This business strategy is in no way reprehensible – it represents a very successful export effort (the *Financial Times* has won the Queen's award for exports). But it gives a further twist to the specialized and politically unrepresentative character of these papers' readership, and makes it all the more necessary to complement them with newspapers of equivalent quality and a readership base more representative of the domestic electorate.

8. The newspapers that survive

Discussions of the characteristics of the press frequently get off on the wrong trail by the false assumption that a newspaper is a kind of public service organization run by journalists in pursuit of the higher truth and in the interests of an ever-expanding body of informed readers. Remarkably, a discussion along these lines was held by the American Economic Association[10] in 1971 under the chairmanship of Walter Heller, who was chief economic adviser to President Kennedy. Newspapers are business enterprises, or parts of larger businesses. As such, their managements aim, in some measure and in some combination, to maximize profits, growth and security, and to do the latter through diversification and the spreading of risks.

Are newspapers run as businesses? The usual rejoinder is that they are not. Either because they are regarded as a public service, or because they are seen as incompetent. But one may refer to an ingenious analytical device used by economists of the Chicago school – the 'as if' hypothesis: whether or not all firms maximize profits, the ones that come closest to operating *as if* they maximize profits will be the firms that survive. The newspaper managements that come closest to rational business behaviour will be the newspapers that survive.

In a letter to the *New Statesman*[11] a Thomson journalist told a story of how during a visit to Russia his boss had concerned himself not at all with the editorial coverage of the visit, but had sat on a Crimean beach with a foot rule measuring the column inches of *Sunday Times* advertisements. Presumably if the measure had revealed an unsatisfactory total, Thomson's interest in the editorial department would have been reawakened.

In newspapers whose management and finances are governed by effective trusts, the editorial objectives of the paper have a more prominent place. The Scott family trust which controls *The Guardian*, the strongest trust arrangement in British newspaper history, holds all the ordinary shares in the group, and the trustees draw no dividends. The objective of management is to support the editorial function, rather than the other way round.

Yet while such an arrangement can be a cushion against adversity, it can provide no lasting protection against continuing financial losses. Thus the transformation of other papers into trusts of comparable type, while no doubt desirable on a number of grounds, would not change the commercial realities confronting those papers. Commercial viability was not assured by the trust status of the pre-Thomson *Times*.

References

1 WINTOUR, Charles, *Pressures on the Press*, André Deutsch, 1972, p. 42.

2 WILES, Peter, 'Pilkington and the Theory of Value', *Economic Journal*, June 1963.

3 KRISTOL, Irving, 'Capitalism, Socialism and Nihilism', *The Public Interest*, Spring 1973.

4 BRITTAN, Samuel, 'Politics and Markets', *The Banker*, October 1973, p. 1116.

5 TUNSTALL, Jeremy, *Journalists at Work*, Constable, 1971, pages 121–22.

6 SEYMOUR-URE, Colin, *The Political Impact of Mass Media*, Constable, 1974, p. 264.

7 *The Sunday Times*, 19 May 1974.

8 *The Sunday Times Magazine*, 12 November 1972.

9 The lobbying was described with great frankness by Uwe KITZINGER in *Diplomacy and Persuasion*, Thames and Hudson, 1973, Chapter 7.

10 *American Economic Review, Papers and Proceedings*, May 1972.

11 Letter from David Leitch, *New Statesman*, 3 November 1972.

4 What is white, black and red all over?

The Times is read by the people who run the country.
The Guardian is read by the people who would like to run the country.
The *Financial Times* is read by the people who own the country.
The Daily Telegraph is read by the people who remember the country as it used to be.
The *Daily Express* is read by the people who think the country is still like that.
The *Daily Mail* is read by the wives of the men who run the country.
The *Daily Mirror* (which itself once tried to run the country) is read by the people who think they run the country.
The *Morning Star* is read by the people who would like another country to run the country.
The Sun – well, Murdoch has found a gap in the market – the oldest gap in the world.

An advertising copywriter

In the bowels of newspaper production departments, among the men that run the machines and among the managers who are meant to oversee them, there is deep insecurity. Wolf has often been cried. Nearly always the wolf has not turned up. But there is a fatalistic conviction that he will get in – eventually. And since he is coming, they may as well get what they can until then. This insecurity helps explain why it is so difficult to bring about the changes that are necessary for survival, the sort of changes that any business in any industry continually has to make. Insecurity shows up in an inflexible attitude to manning levels, wage rates, the introduction of new technology and new working methods. Inflexibility in turn makes it almost impossible to overcome the perpetual rise in costs by increasing productivity. Unable to make the production machine more efficient, newspaper managements have been forced to fuel it with more and more revenue. Cover prices have gone up, partly because of the dramatic rise in newsprint costs, but partly beyond that. Newspapers have all tried to grab more advertising revenue – those able to do so have edged upmarket to get it.

Newspapers do a delicate scissors dance. While the revenue blade holds steady, the cost blade chops profits into losses; then, for a time, the cost blade stays still and the revenue blade opens things up, thanks to a rise in cover prices or advertising. Newspapers fluctuate in and out of profit rapidly. Since a 1p rise in the cover price of the *Daily Express* brings in a revenue of about £6 million, this can at a stroke eradicate the loss of £3 million at which the paper was running in 1973. With a quality newspaper, the changes in advertising cause similar bonanzas, or havocs; and such fluctuations periodically afflict the press as a whole, as advertising is among the most sensitive reflectors of the state of business confidence. This is one explanation for the phenomenon of periodic crisis that afflicts Fleet Street. Up in arms one minute, talk of redundancies, closures, imminent disaster; up in the clouds the next as the situation suddenly recovers. Thus it is that newspaper managements find it hard to convince themselves or their workers that radical change is necessary.

One way or another, the newspapers struggle on. The record of death, closure and rationalization is regularly rehearsed, not least by journalists. Yet it is far less bloody than, say, that of aerospace, or of computers, or of package holidays – or of other would-be growth industries like fringe banking and life assurance. The only national newspaper to close during the 1950s was the *Sunday Chronicle* (1955). In the 1960s the death toll was heavy among the Sundays: *Sunday Graphic* (1960), *Sunday Dispatch*

(1961), *Empire News* (1960), *Reynolds News* (1966). None of these could claim to be a product of the higher editorial art. The hybrid daily, the *News Chronicle*, part quality, part popular, went in 1960; the first *Sun* rose from the ashes of the *Daily Herald* in 1964; in 1969 the second and very different *Sun* was born. In 1971 the *Daily Sketch* was merged into the *Daily Mail*, another newspaper in the Associated Newspapers group. The only net addition was the *Sunday Telegraph* in 1961. Its running losses are a warning to anyone rash enough to launch a newspaper.

In 1973 the national daily newspapers sold about eleven million copies a day, got £99 million from their readers and £94 million from their advertisers. The national Sundays sold an average of twenty-two million copies for the one day a week, got £43 million from their readers and £42 million from their advertisers. This adds up to an industry worth £280 million a year. For comparison, this is a third more than the combined income of the commercial television companies. Including all the colour supplements and surveys, which accounted for about £17 million in the exceptionally good year of 1973, the qualities got £44 million from display and financial advertising, about £33 million from classified advertising and just under £30 million from their readers. Table 4.1 shows the trend of the sums spent on national newspapers, although these include advertising agents' commissions and newsagents' discounts.

The celebrated decline of newspapers does not show up in many of the indicators by which the fate and fortunes of industries are measured. In 1966, the public spent £109 million on buying their newspapers, and seven years later almost twice as much in money terms. This is the annual accumulation of all those daily pennies (unlike the circulation revenue figures in the previous paragraph, they include the discounts that the newsagents and wholesalers keep, which works out at about 35 per cent of the cover price). In real terms, that is after allowing for inflation which makes money an ever-worse measuring rod of change, the increase in the public's spending on newspapers was much smaller but still substantial, at 28 per cent. A better way of judging how much the public valued newspapers is to look at the percentage of people's spending that goes on them, rather than at the raw money sums. As a proportion of all consumers' expenditures, out of every £1 spent by consumers, a fairly constant 0·4p or thereabouts, or just under one half of 1 per cent, has gone on national newspapers in every year since 1958 (which is as far back as we have looked). In 1971 and in 1972, the proportion even went up

Table 4.1 Money spent on national newspapers

	1968 £m	1969 £m	1970 £m	1971 £m	1972 £m	1973 £m	1968–73 average annual increase %
Advertising							
Display	68	76	75	76	85	104	8·9
Classified	22	26	25	22	29	41	13·3
Financial	9	9	8	10	16	15	10·8
	99	111	108	108	130	160	10·1
Sales	129	131	151	182	202	208	10·0
	228	242	259	290	332	368	10·0

Advertising before advertising agents' commission, sales before distribution discount. Source: Advertising Association, estimates.

slightly: in those years consumers spent ½p out of every £1 on newspapers. A truly declining industry, like the film industry for example, gets an ever smaller proportion of people's spending. But newspapers have been able to put up their cover prices and get away with it. They have won a sufficient claim on the affections and purses of their readers.

The question for each newspaper is how best to survive the scissors dance; which formula is most successful in putting up the revenue, or, with luck, holding down the costs. The scissors analogy is, in fact, deceptively simple. It is not just that costs and

The link between costs & revenues

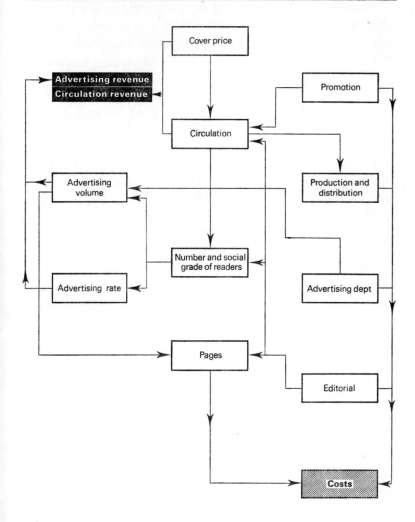

Adapted from 'How research can help get the price right', by Alan Wolfe and Peter Bartram, a paper delivered to The European Society for Opinion and Market Research Conference, November 1972.

revenues are interrelated, but most individual costs and separate sources of revenue interact on each other. The main relationships are illustrated in the chart above.

Advertising revenue, for example, depends on the volume of advertising and the advertising rate. The volume of advertising depends both on having enough salesmen to go out and get the ads and on the number and social grade of readers. The more ads they pull in, the more has to be spent on newsprint to accommodate them. And since reputable newspapers keep a proper balance between the number of pages devoted to advertisements and to editorial, a higher number of advertising pages means more editorial pages, and thus higher editorial costs. The advertising rate is a result both of circulation and of the spending calibre of the readers, as explained in Chapter Three. The more upmarket the editorial, the higher the social grade of readership, and the higher the advertising rates.

Table 4.2 Cost structures compared

	Times	*Financial Times*	*Daily Mirror*	*Sunday Times*	*Sunday People*	*Sunday Mirror*
		Cost items as % of direct costs				
Editorial	22·0	21·6	15·2	12·4	13·4	15·3
Newsprint	20·4	14·5	40·0	28·7	30·2	32·2
Production	38·0	37·9	28·7	41·1	40·6	35·4
Distribution and selling	19·6	26·0	16·1	17·8	15·8	17·1
	100·0	100·0	100·0	100·0	100·0	100·0
		Costs per copy sold, pence				
Editorial	2·33	3·57	0·33	2·71	0·59	0·63
Newsprint	2·14	2·39	0·87	6·26	1·34	1·32
Production	4·02	6·25	0·63	8·96	1·80	1·46
Distribution and selling	2·07	4·28	0·35	3·90	0·70	0·70
	10·56	16·49	2·18	21·83	4·43	4·11

Source: Appendix; figures for calendar 1973 or year to March 1974.

The resulting contrasts in the structures of costs and revenues of quality newspapers vis-à-vis populars are reflected in the figures supplied to us by certain newspapers – other newspaper managements upheld the reticence that has obliged even Royal Commissions to aggregate individual results into group totals. Our summary analysis in table 4.2 (the detailed figures are in the Appendix) show that in 1973–4 the average direct costs of producing the *Daily Mirror*, in terms of each copy sold, was 2.2p. This compared with 10.6p for *The Times* and 16.5p for the *Financial Times* in 1973, when the *Financial Times* received 4.6p net per copy from its cover price of 7p. But the *FT* obtained advertising revenue nine-tenths as large as the *Daily Mirror*, for one-twentieth the circulation (see Appendix). Those costs directly related to circulation – mainly newsprint and some distribution costs – are correspondingly lower in total; and this provides scope for relatively larger resources to be devoted to editorial and also to selling and publicity costs. Thus the *Financial Times* can profitably devote more than ten times as much per copy sold to editorial expenses as the *Daily Mirror;* which is the economic basis of its unrivalled stable of specialist writers.

Because quality papers typically lose money in the first instance on each additional copy sold, they make money from extra sales only where these go to readers who are interesting to advertisers. The advertisers are more concerned by the composition of the readership of a quality than by its size. With the populars, the size of the circulation is more important, but they are more vulnerable to increase in costs. Newsprint forms 40 per cent of the costs of the *Daily Mirror*, so a rise in the price of newsprint is more significant than at *The Times* where newsprint is a fifth of costs, or at the *Financial Times* where newsprint comprises only 15 per cent.

The cost and revenue ingredients for newspapers are mixed together to produce a different result for each paper and each group of newspapers. If the hugely expensive rotary presses can be used seven days a week to produce a daily, a Sunday and an evening paper, then clearly the economies will be greater than if the presses stand idle for hours or days. This helps to explain the very wide range of costs and profits found within the various categories of newspapers. The 1970 report of the National Board for Prices and Incomes[1] found that among the qualities, newsprint costs fell in a range of 19 to 34 per cent of all costs, editorial costs 12 to 23 per cent and production costs 24 to 33 per cent. The range of production costs for the populars was narrower, from 27 to 30 per cent, but of editorial costs was 13 to 24 per cent of the total. These figures are not strictly comparable with those in the Appendix; for the relevant past years, we show newsprint costs rather lower and production costs higher.

Broadly what seems to have been happening to newspapers is that the scissors movements of costs and revenue have been continually pushing up the break-even points of newspapers. That is, cost pressures in excess of general inflation have forced newspapers to collect ever more revenue, either by putting up their prices faster than inflation, or by getting more for advertising. The uneasy question for newspapers is whether they are eventually going to hit a ceiling on revenues so that rising costs force them out of business. The key factor here has long been the inability of managements to overcome the fear of production workers of accepting cost-saving changes in both technology and organization. As this book went to press in January, Fleet Street was in the throes of yet another industrial dispute, at a time when such disputes could shut some newspapers down permanently.

The economics of mass circulations and low cover prices were first put into practice by Alfred Harmsworth, who became Lord Northcliffe. When Northcliffe founded the *Daily Mail* in 1896, its price was ½d, as against 1d charged by other popular newspapers. On day one it sold 397 215 copies. Using the new, faster Linotype method of setting and casting type (brought in against union opposition) and the excellent national train services that ran from London, he was able to get wide breakfast-time circulation. Four years later the *Daily Mail* was printed in Manchester too, and the circulation went up to nearly one million. The paper was deliberately designed to appeal to a wide range of interests.

Northcliffe took advantage of the simple fact that half the population was composed of women and initiated special features aimed at them.

Thus began the era of cheap national newspapers – or, rather, nationally distributed London newspapers – which allied the advertisers' pounds to the readers' pennies to create slick, well-produced 'popular' newspapers, but entirely different from the popular paper as exemplified by William Cobbett's *Political Register* of seventy-five years earlier, which played a part in making working people more politically aware and active.

Northcliffe introduced the idea of audited sales certificates to satisfy the advertisers that they were being given value for money. Henry Wickham Steed, editor of *The Times* from 1919 to 1922, complained in 1938 that had Northcliffe lived to see the consequences, he would have regretted them.

None knew better than he that an advertisement-ridden Press cannot be a free press. He was convinced that the Press, if it wished to preserve its own independence, must keep advertisers in their proper places as salesmen, and not allow them to dictate policy or even to vulgarize the appearance of a newspaper by glaring 'display' advertisements. He failed to see that the mania of 'net sales certificates' would end by giving large buyers of newspaper publicity the whip-hand of journalism by making the Press a handmaid of 'big business'.[2]

This was written at the end of a decade of explosion in the circulations of newspapers as, for business reasons, the newspapers fought to assemble ever bigger audiences for their advertisers. After a time, the circulation battle became an end in itself, with the newspaper proprietors vying with each other to get the biggest certified net daily sale. The battle was between the *Daily Herald* – which started it all off – and the *Daily Mail*, the *Daily Express* and the *News Chronicle*. The weapons were free insurance, aluminium cooking pots and sets of the complete works of Charles Dickens and other authors. At the fiercest, these papers were spending £60 000 a week (equivalent to £300 000 in 1974 money) on promotion.

The *Daily Herald* had been launched with £300 in 1912 (try starting a newspaper with £1600 in 1974). It was founded by

George Lansbury who designed it as the conscience of the Labour movement. Its history is important because it illustrates the barriers that a paper whose constituency is among Labour Party supporters has to overcome. It was plagued by financial problems throughout its life. In 1922, the Trades Union Congress and the National Executive Committee of the Labour Party assumed responsibility for it, but the financial troubles continued. Seven years later Odhams, the magazine publishers and printers, bought 51 per cent, leaving 49 per cent with the TUC, and editorial control with an editorial board. Lord Southwood, the chairman of Odhams, was keen to have a daily newspaper using the presses of the *Sunday People* during the week, and he introduced new marketing touches. Party members who brought in 100 new readers were given £3 15s for themselves and had £2 10s put into party funds. The circulation went up to one million. Southwood threw himself wholeheartedly into the freewheeling promotional battle. He succeeded in boosting circulation to two million – but the only enduring result was to bind the plays of George Bernard Shaw into one volume given away to new subscribers. When the war and newsprint rationing ended the nonsense, a long slow decline in circulation set in that reached 1·7 million in 1955 and 1·4 million in 1960. The readers that did stay loyal were the 'wrong' sort, containing a higher proportion of men readers (nearly three-fifths) than any other national, the lowest percentage of housewives, the highest percentage of C2 and DE readers. The biggest single loss had been among the young, leaving a high percentage of older readers. Odhams' surveys showed that the readers had strong feelings about the paper and read it with greater intensity than people read other non-qualities. They were the underpaid and underprivileged who resented the way society had treated them and felt that the *Herald* sympathized with them. In 1961 the Daily Mirror group (which became a part of the International Publishing Corporation) bought Odhams, and inherited the *Herald*, promising to keep it alive for seven years. By the early 1960s, its traditional cloth cap attitudes did not fit in at all with the image younger Labour voters were being offered by Harold Wilson, a garb more attractive to advertisers.

The *Mirror* people had been very rude about the *Herald* in their written evidence to the Shawcross Commission on why it failed; they said 'The pudding appeared in the (Labour) *Herald*, and the sauce in the (Labour) *Daily Mirror*'.[3] They were given the chance to sauce it up. Hugh Cudlipp had shown that a Labour paper, independent of the party, could thrive if its journalism was brash and imaginative enough. As it told the Commission, what was needed was a vigorous approach . . . 'Only journalism of an outstandingly original level will reverse the present trend – journalism backed by skilful promotion'.[4] Mark Abrams, the market research expert who believed that affluence would turn the old working class bourgeois, was engaged to look ahead to the next ten years of the newspaper reading public. He pointed out that by the end of the decade, half the population would be under thirty-five and the preoccupations of this new generation would be entirely different from those of the old (*Daily Herald*) generation. The members of the new generation would be better-educated than the old, less class conscious and would expect a high and rising standard of living; they would live in good houses, have cars and expect to travel. Their political outlook would be, as Cecil King, IPC's chairman said, 'secular rather than ideological and critical rather than undiscriminating',[5] and they would vote for whoever promised competence in social engineering – the provision of better homes, schools, cities. Consumer politics were seen to displace ideological politics.

For the sake of these new consumers, euthanasia was delivered to the *Daily Herald*, and, on 15 September 1964 the *Sun* rose to shine on an election campaign that was to return Harold Wilson's first government. But something went wrong. The Mirror Group reckoned the paper would pay its way with a circulation of 1.7 million. In 1965 its daily average reached only 1.3 million, which is what the *Herald* had sold in 1963. For seven years the *Sun* hung like an albatross round the neck of IPC, until it was handed over to News International, the company of Rupert Murdoch, in 1969. Politics went, naked ladies arrived, and the circulation soared.

Tracing the history of newspapers through the decades brings

c

home the strength of the cliché that newspapers have to change with the times. And the most important things about newspapers are not the way they look, or what size they are, or how well they are marketed, but what is in them – and how well-off their readers are. The *Herald* failed to hang on to enough of its traditional readers to be economically viable, a number which had to be high since they were the less affluent members of the community. It made a deliberate attempt to adapt to what the market researchers told it was the new audience. It failed. But its stablemate, the *Daily Mirror*, had proved that a paper for the workers could not only survive but be extraordinarily profitable if enough workers bought it. The difference between the *Mirror* and the *Herald* may have been that the one had the journalism of Hugh Cudlipp and the other did not; the difference between the Murdoch *Sun* and the IPC *Sun* was that Murdoch's paper was recognizably distinct from the brand leader, the *Daily Mirror*. The economies of scale which are at their greatest with papers with the huge circulation of the *Mirror* make it almost impossible for another paper aimed at the working-class market to break in unless it is radically different. Murdoch relied on a not quite new form of aggression, the naked variety – and it worked.

When the *News Chronicle* folded in 1961, it had a circulation of 1.2 million. Just after the Second World War the circulation had been one-third higher. The explanation for its decline given in evidence by the company to the Shawcross Commission was that the paper could not compete with the mass papers for working-class advertising, nor with the qualities for upmarket advertising. But there are also grounds for the report's comment that 'different and more consistent managerial and editorial policy might have saved this newspaper'. The *News Chronicle* and its London evening stablemate *The Star* were never very profitable, and the *News Chronicle* and its predecessor the *Daily News* were wedded to the then declining fortunes of the Liberal party. It would not, as it explained in its evidence, desert 'the mass audience for the possibly safer haven of an audience entirely in the comfortable classes' nor make 'the compromises with principle and good taste that might have enabled it to secure a larger popular circulation'.[6] Like the Liberal Party, it fell betwixt and between. The management admitted that it failed to change its 'formula' as newsprint restrictions were progressively lifted and the newspapers with the money increased their sizes and coverage. The advertisers went to the big spenders, leaving the *Chronicle* a thin twelve pages. Costs rose above the break-even point, and the management could not stem the momentum of decline.

There has to be a rough coalescence between what the public wants and what the proprietors want to give it. Lord Beaverbrook clearly enjoyed boasting that 'I ran the paper purely for the purpose of making propaganda, and with no other purpose. . . . But in order to make propaganda effective the paper had to be successful. No paper is any good at all for propaganda unless it has a thoroughly good financial position.'[7] This deliberate attempt to shock succeeded, though what he said is not a fair summary of his approach to his own newspapers. His meaning of propaganda was not simply his long and extraordinary campaign for Empire Free Trade, which had hardly any effect, but that a newspaper should in its leader columns and by the selection of its news take a firm declamatory stance. He wanted his papers profitable, so that he could carry on declaiming, but he did not want the shareholders to see the money. The dividend policy of Beaverbrook Newspapers was miserly, and half of the profits went to the Beaverbrook Foundations and from thence to art galleries and retired Presbyterian ministers in Canada. He was bored by the running of his businesses and left it to others. To Tom Blackburn, then chairman of the *Daily Express*, he wrote in 1964, just before he died: 'the last time I looked at your balance sheet reserves it stood at £1 million but now there is only £600 000. Where did the rest go?'[8] That is not a question Lord Thomson would ever have asked. Moreover Beaverbrook scanned the balance sheets and complained when the newspapers made too much money.

The widespread fear of press barons, generated by Northcliffe and Rothermere, and in a rather different way by Beaverbrook, is now largely an anachronism. Their passing has indeed removed one source of diversity, but there is on balance little reason to lament it. A. J. P. Taylor's sentimental defence of Beaverbrook, the man and the tycoon, only confirms – thanks to Taylor's scruples as a historian – the abuses his hero visited on his newspapers and readers. These started from the puffs the rising MP bought for himself with his first investment in the *Daily Express*, went on to black lists that indeed existed, and included orders to avoid criticism of a cabinet minister whose wife Beaverbrook loved. He used to dictate messages into a Soundscriber and dispatch them to the paper: 'We have a system you know. I speak at this end and there is a machine at the other end and it comes out as a leading article.'[9] How charmingly impish it is in retrospect, and how tyrannical and soul-destroying it was at the time.

There is no baron in sight who would make a claim comparable to that Rothermere made to Beaverbrook in 1922: 'If Bonar (Law) places himself in my hands I will hand him down to posterity at the end of three years as one of the most successful Prime Ministers in history, and if there is a general election I will get him returned again. This may sound boastful but I know exactly how it can be done.'[10] The part played by the *Daily Mail* in the Zinoviev letter episode suggests that these claims were more than eccentricities. Today instead there is the continual pressure to conform to the dictates of the marketplace, and to find the right formula.

The formula on which the *Daily Express* and *Sunday Express* grew prosperous was to appeal to all classes. As Beaverbrook said in one of a series of articles on the aims of the *Daily Express* in 1937: 'The *Daily Express* is the first newspaper to serve every class in the community, rich and poor, high and low, barbarian, Scythian, bond and free.'[11] And while the circulation carried on rising, the formula was as brilliant a success as the paper's finances. As circulation rose, so did both circulation and advertising revenue. And costs. Beaverbrook was the last of the big spenders, who actively believed in paying high wages. The *Daily Express* reached its peak average daily circulation in 1961, with 4·3 million a day. Twelve years and one million fewer a day later, the financial pips started squeaking: the costs of reaching so many people in all classes became greater than the benefits. Television did the job more cheaply.

It is ironic that the four papers that had taken part in the circulation battle of the dailies in the 1930s either perished or came near the danger line by the early 1970s. During the Second World War and for many years after, newsprint rationing prevented the forces of competition from killing off the weaker papers. Once newsprint became freely available – which was not until 1958 – advertising in the popular press moved to the papers with the cheapest costs per thousand readers, as they could afford to run more pages to accommodate the advertisements that had been deflected to the weaker sisters. But then the competition from television started eating into the stronger brethren. The circulations came down, and advertisers turned more and more to television to reach the broad mass of the public. However, there was another reason for the declines in the populars' circulations.

Since the ending of restrictions on newsprint consumption, newspapers have been getting fatter. One effect of this has been that people have changed their reading habits. Instead of buying several thin papers, they have, in the case of the populars, bought fewer fatter papers. It is this decline which is associated in peoples' minds with the decline of the industry. But as James Curran has pointed out[12] the number of newspapers sold is a very imperfect measure of the performance of the newspaper industry; it is rather like measuring the performance of a restaurant by counting up the number of meals served, a measure that does not take account of how much people eat of what, or of how much they spend. Looking instead at the number of pages sold, or (as we have seen) at the amount of money the public is prepared to spend on newspapers, a different picture presents itself. As the papers got fatter, they started new sections and features to appeal more to women, to the young, to business readers, to sports fans, to gardeners and home decorators, to savers and just plain news hounds. Each paper set out to be the compleat newspaper. Comparing the average sizes of newspapers in the months of January and February 1974 with the sizes in

The dailies average circulation each publishing day

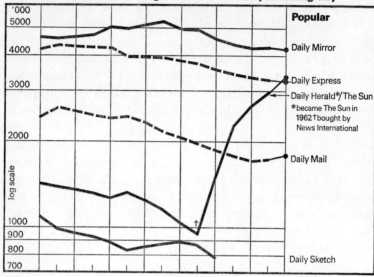

Popular

'000
5000
4000
3000
2000
1000
900
800
700

log scale

Daily Mirror
Daily Express
Daily Herald*/The Sun
*became The Sun in 1962 †bought by News International
Daily Mail
Daily Sketch

†

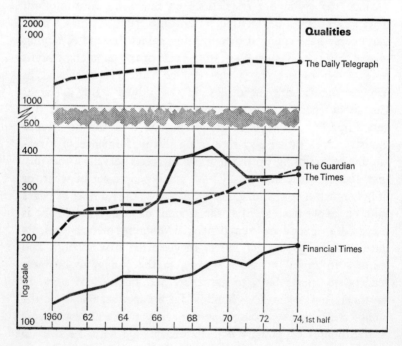

Qualities

2000
'000
1000
500
400
300
200
100

log scale

The Daily Telegraph
The Guardian
The Times
Financial Times

1960   62   64   66   68   70   72   74, 1st half

The Sundays average circulation each publishing day

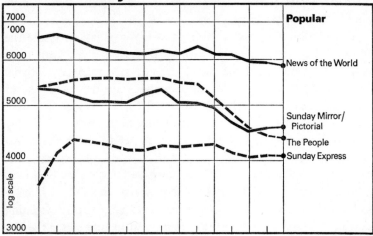

Popular

- 7000
- '000
- 6000 — News of the World
- 5000 — Sunday Mirror/ Pictorial
- The People
- 4000 — Sunday Express
- log scale
- 3000

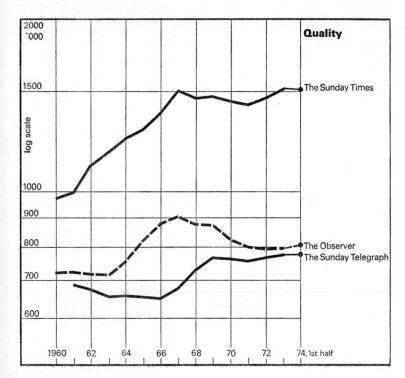

Quality

- 2000
- '000
- log scale
- 1500 — The Sunday Times
- 1000
- 900
- 800 — The Observer
- The Sunday Telegraph
- 700
- 600

1960   62   64   66   68   70   72   74, 1st half

those months twelve years earlier, table 4.3 shows that the *Daily Express* was, for example, 25 per cent bigger, and the *Daily Mirror* almost 50 per cent bigger.

The qualities got fatter without losing circulation. Quite the reverse. The circulations of nearly all the qualities, both daily and Sunday, increased steadily. This is because rising educational levels and increasing affluence bumped up the numbers of potential AB readers, who, as part of their AB way of life, have felt inclined, or obliged, to take a quality newspaper.

The *Financial Times* hit the most successful formula: a low circulation (giving it particularly low newsprint costs), but a very select readership. This is composed largely of business-men and managers in the public sector who are not only unusually well off themselves but who also command very large purchasing power. There is a total coalition of interest in that editorially the newspaper wants to reach the audience that is most lucrative for advertisers – in contrast with, say, the case with *The Guardian*. The *Financial Times* aims at and achieves excellence in the reporting of economics, industry, politics, world affairs and the arts. Somehow the same searching and critical zeal is not directed at the business of the City and of individual firms. As far as its own backyard is concerned, the *FT* retains the inoffensive character of a trade or local paper. This pattern is a direct outcome of the formula for the paper's financial success established under the management of Lord Drogheda and the two-decade editorship (superbly successful by its own standards) of Sir Gordon Newton: the formula of news reporting that businessmen cannot afford to miss, as a basis for a vast expansion of financial and industrial advertising from all over the world. The *Financial Times* reports the facts about industrial disputes without the anti-strike bias common in other papers. The *Financial Times* readers do not 'need the pro-employer bias since they are on the side of the employer already'.[13] Businessmen need facts about economic trends and political developments on which to base their decisions, and this encourages unslanted reporting; ideology they can get from the *Daily Telegraph*. Individual firms and City institutions are not put under the same searchlight. This would be a quick way of alienating the businessmen on whom the paper's financial strength, and thereby its professional excellence, depend. It might also on occasion be embarrassing for the rest of the vast Cowdray financial empire of which the *Financial Times*, owned by S. Pearson, is only a part.

The *Financial Times* identifies not so much with capitalists as with managers: with the people who happen to be in charge. Its mission is not to convert its readers but to help them run their firms, their departments and their personal finances. Some seek to change the world; others to understand it; the *Financial Times* rides it. First class, of course. In homage to this instinct, an aficionado fantasized on the *Financial Times* leader that would follow a communist revolution in Britain.

The new government has come to office by an unorthodox route, which in itself has set an unfortunate precedent; and a number of its specific policy proposals will require much closer attention. But even a red cloud has a silver lining. At least the period of uncertainty is at an end. What is necessary now is to strengthen the hand of the moderate factions in the government, centred on the Trotskyite Syndicalists. Responsible leaders in industry and the City . . .

Running a successful newspaper is a matter of getting the formula right. This the *Financial Times* has achieved to the envy of its less successful rivals. This would not have been possible without good management and skilful editorship; but neither would it have been possible if the formula had been a more demanding one than selling to the best-heeled readers available.

Success, and failure, in getting the formula right are both illustrated by The Thomson Organization. In 1959, Lord Thomson gained control of the Kemsley regional newspapers and of *The Sunday Times*, whose circulation was 879 000. With flair, panache and loads of long memoirs, its circulation rose speedily to one million in 1961. In February of that year, *The Sunday Times Magazine*, in glorious colour, was launched free to all prepared to pay the price of the paper (7d, or nearly 3p). The circulation shot up by nearly 20 per cent. More important, there was no significant 'dilution' of readership: the extra copies went mostly to A and B readers.

Table 4·3 Newspaper groups

	Sales m copies 1962	1974	Pages Jan/Feb 1962	1974	Price p 1962	Dec 1974	1p increase raises‡ £m	Readership % AB (13)	C1 (23)	(All Adults) C2 (33)	DE (31)
Public companies											
Associated Newspapers											
Profit £9·6m Mar 1974											
*Daily Mail**	2·6	1·8	13·1	35·8*	1·25	5	3·2	16	31	29	25
Evening News	1·4	0·8	—	—	1·25	4	1·6	14	26	34	25
Beaverbrook Newspapers											
Loss £1.4m June 1974											
Daily Express	4·3	3·2	13·6	17·1	1·25	5	6·1	15	28	31	27
Sunday Express	4·5	4·1	29·5	32·0	2·08	8	1·3	22	32	27	19
Evening Standard	0·7	0·5	—	—	1·25	4	1·0	23	33	27	17
News International											
Profit £10·3m Dec 1973											
The Sun†	1·3	3·3	11·4	30·0	1·25	5	5·4	5	18	43	35
News of the World	6·6	5·9	20·2	23·5	2·50	6	1·8	5	17	40	38
Pearson Longman											
Profit £14·7m Dec 1973											
Financial Times	0·1	0·2	19·4	34·8	1·67	8	0·4	47	34	11	8
Reed International§											
Profit £65·5m Mar 1974											
Daily Mirror	4·6	4·2	22·1	32·2	1·25	5	8·0	5	19	42	35

Sunday Mirror¶ ‖	5·2	4·6	33·0	46·0	2·08	6	1·4	6	21	42	32
Sunday People	5·5	4·4	22·2	22·0	2·50	6	1·4	6	19	40	36

Thomson Organization
Profit £13·5m Dec 1973

The Times	0·2	0·4	21·0	28·7	2·08	8	0·6	50	28	13	9
The Sunday Times	1·1	1·5	43·5	66·0	2·92	12	0·5	41	33	18	9

Private companies
The Daily Telegraph
Profit £3·0m Mar 1973

The Daily Telegraph	1·3	1·4	20·9	29·3	1·25	6	2·6	42	35	14	10
Sunday Telegraph	0·7	0·8	27·5	37·5	2·08	8	0·3	39	33	17	11

Guardian and Manchester Evening News
Profit £2·2m Mar 1973

The Guardian	0·2	0·4	16·7	23·5	1·67	8	0·6	40	36	16	9

The Observer
Profit £0·8m Dec 1973

The Observer	0·7	0·8	38·5	37·8	2·5	10	0·3	35	36	20	10

---

* Merged with *Daily Sketch* and became tabloid in 1971.
† Successor to *Daily Herald* which ceased publication in 1964.
‡ Effect of increasing prices by 1p is after deducting newsagents' and wholesalers' discount and assumes no loss of circulation.
§ Took over IPC in May 1970.
¶ Was called *Sunday Pictorial*.
Profits are pre-tax profits for financial years ending in month shown.
Sources: *The Economist*, 6 April 1974, updated; JICNARS National Readership Survey July 1973–June 1974.

Even more important, an additional source of revenue had been opened up. Advertisers were offered more middle-class readers and a new outlet to appeal to them in. Ever since then, *The Sunday Times* has increased its circulation in spite of frequent price rises. This success seems to have been achieved at the cost of the paper's old rival *The Observer*. As the readers waded through an ever larger *Sunday Times*, with more and more sections and supplements, when it came to axeing items from the newsagents' monthly bill, *The Observer* suffered, even though for much of the time it was selling at a cheaper cover price than *The Sunday Times*.

But *The Times* was a different story. Lord Thomson gained control of *The Times* in 1966 and promised a sceptical Monopolies Commission that his group would retain its independence (the reference to that Commission was the result of a recommendation by the 1962 Royal Commission report that press amalgamations should be scrutinized). Thomson thought that the marketing techniques which worked with *The Sunday Times* could be transferred to *The Times*, and Denis Hamilton, editor-in-chief of *The Sunday Times*, extended his function to cover *The Times* too and transferred his base of operations to Printing House Square. But what was sauce for the Sunday goose was not sauce for the daily gander. Sunday papers and daily papers are different. The Sundays are a leisurely read and depend heavily on the quality of the features for their appeal. By physically splitting up *The Sunday Times*, it was possible to appeal to different groups among the vast readership – women, car enthusiasts, teenagers – separately, and the sheer bulk of the paper made it feel like good value for money. It was possible to put on circulation in huge dollops. A daily newspaper has to rely on news. People have less time to read and are not therefore overjoyed at a thick paper full of features. But *The Times* sprouted a business news section. It sprouted a Saturday Weekend Review section. It stopped looking like a serious newspaper with thunder in its lines. (The same marketing error was made in reverse by the dull-looking but newsy *Daily Telegraph* when it started a Sunday version which looked and read like the seventh day edition of the daily.)

The Times slid downmarket on an expensive spiral. It went all out for circulation, and got it: from a circulation of 256 000 in 1965, it rose by a vast 69 per cent to 432 000 four years later. The extra readers were bought expensively and they were not of the same social class as the existing readers. The total of readers – including new cohorts of C1, C2 and even Ds and Es – reached three quarters of a million in 1969, and brought the percentage of ABs down to only 43 per cent. The effective advertising cost per thousand of ABs went up, and the advertisers did not turn to *The Times* in the requisite force. The promotional campaign continued along lines which were bizarre from the advertising point of view, emphasizing that *The Times* was not exclusive, was not for Top People – was not the things that made it such a good medium for display and classified advertising. Market economics dictate that unless a quality newspaper makes a profit per copy sold to its readers, which is extremely unlikely, each extra reader must have advertising appeal. By 1971 the policy was reversed and new management brought in. Duke Hussey came from Associated Newspapers to become managing director of Times Newspapers. *The Times* became sober again, the business section was incorporated back into the paper so that when the news warranted it, business stories hit the front page. The Saturday Review became much truncated. Untrendy once more, *The Times* dropped the excess C2s and lower ranks and the circulation dropped back to a base of 340 000 in 1972 from which it could build up again as new members join the AB club, but gradually. By June 1974, the ABs were again 50 per cent of the readership, and in 1973 the loss on *The Times*, after deducting administration and overheads, was a mere £187 000; in 1971, it had been £1·4 million. *The Times* is a classic example of the necessity for a newspaper to get all the elements of the formula right if it wants to make a profit, or keep its losses down: an increase in circulation, which seems such a natural objective for a newspaper, proved treacherous since it threw the delicate interrelationships of costs and different kinds of revenues out of balance.

Even when *The Times* was back 'in balance' with half its readership solidly among the ABs, it made a loss in 1973, a year when the advertising was flowing like honey. How can a paper carry on losing money like this year after year? The generosity of Lord Thomson and his family is often cited as the reason, which does not quite square with his celebrated business attitude to newspapers. There is certainly an element of 'colonial boy makes good and conquers the heights of the British establishment' about Thomson, and in that respect he takes after Beaverbrook, another Canadian. There is also more to it. The Thomson empire is financially set up so that the losses of *The Times* are not unduly painful. In the first place, although *The Times* makes a loss, the other publications with *The Times* prefix – the *Literary Supplement* and *Educational Supplement* and the world atlases – are profitable so that all the The Times publications together make a profit. And then the specific losses of *The Times* are extracted from The Thomson Organization so that they do not depress its share price. They are borne by Thomson Scottish Associates, a private company controlled by Thomson and his family. TSA has two assets. One is the control of The Thomson Organization, which publishes *The Times* and *The Sunday Times* and regional newspapers, owns the package holidays business, Thomson Travel, and does a few other conglomerate things. The other asset is a slice of North Sea oil. In 1974, Thomson Scottish Associates borrowed the vast sum of £50 million to pay for its share of the exploitation of the oil. The main security given to the bankers was the oil itself, but if everything went disastrously wrong, the bankers would have call on Thomson Scottish Associates' other asset – The Thomson Organization. Thus, indirectly, *The Times* and *The Sunday Times* are pledged to North Sea oil. If the oil is duly profitable, then the newspapers will have a guaranteed cross-subsidy; if it is a disaster, then they would in theory be liable to be put up for sale by the bankers. Not exactly conducive to a clear-sighted editorial view on North Sea oil.

The Times Publishing Company had been controlled by the Hon. Gavin Astor and John Walter, who were not allowed to sell their shares to anyone without the permission of a committee consisting of the Lord Chief Justice of England, the Warden of All Souls College, Oxford, the President of The Royal

Society, the President of the Institute of Chartered Accountants, and the Governor of the Bank of England. This committee of grey eminences had no other function; it was set up to maintain the best traditions and political independence of *The Times* and to eliminate as far as reasonably possible questions of personal ambition or commercial profit. But when the Astor family grew tired of sustaining the paper's losses, the committee decided that Thomson was better than the deep blue sea.

Trust status, whatever its advantages (see p. 55), makes it almost impossible for a newspaper to issue more shares to raise extra capital. The *Observer* had to go through some complicated contortions to secure funds to buy Printing House Square when *The Times* announced its move to *The Sunday Times* offices in Grays Inn Road so that the two Thomson papers could be printed on the same presses. And unless special provisions are enacted for newspaper trusts, they will be subject to the wealth tax. But for all the defects, the Scott Trust that controls the *Manchester Evening News* (the one that makes the profits) and *The Guardian* (the one that gets the prizes) has ensconced public service as the aim of the newspapers in so far as commercial considerations allow. Anyone working for these papers should, according to Alastair Hetherington, the editor of *The Guardian*, 'get down on his hands and knees from time to time, to give thanks for the Scott Trust',[14] a suitably moral posture for *Guardian* journalists.

No one could accuse Lord Hartwell, the proprietor and the editor-in-chief of *The Daily Telegraph* and of the *Sunday Telegraph*, of proclaiming his public service motives on his sleeve. And yet the *Sunday Telegraph* is kept going at a loss because he wants to keep it going. The losses of that paper used to be separately published but they are now submerged in the large profits of *The Daily Telegraph*, which has captured the hearts and minds of middle-class readers and classified advertisers. The Economist Intelligence Unit report of the newspaper industry said in 1966 that the *Telegraph* was the most profitable and least efficient paper in Fleet Street. In the end, inefficiency could be the undoing of the *Telegraph*s. As table 4.1 (on page 60) shows, classified advertising in national newspapers reached £41 million in 1973; for all newspapers together, it reached £220 million. It is the fastest growing form of advertising, exceeding the amount spent on television advertising.

The Telegraph gets about a third of the classifieds that go into national newspapers. But because of a lack of investment in the past, the paper could not increase its size sufficiently to take all the classified ads it was offered, and they spilled over into the pages of other newspapers, like *The Guardian*, trying to establish a niche in classifieds. When a paper becomes the recognized classified market leader for certain kinds of jobs – as is *The Guardian* for engineers and teachers – there is a snowball effect as anyone wanting to advertise for, say, teachers, has to put at least one ad in the pages of the market leader. *The Telegraph* is an example of a newspaper that is profitable but is in danger of losing its touch and its readership unless both editorial and managerial changes are made in good time. Lord Hartwell, sixty-two in 1974, was the chief editor, the chief manager, the chief financial planner, the chief everything. Industrial relations, both with the production workers and with the journalists were somewhat below the low Fleet Street average. The *Daily Telegraph* company was privately owned by Hartwell's family, the Berrys, on whom falls the decision whether or not to invest heavily in new plant and machinery or whether to sell out.

If the *Telegraph* should enter a sticky patch, there is a reserve it can call on: its cover price, which has always been lower than its competitors (and lower than its readers believe, according to research in which newspaper readers were asked how much they thought they were paying for their paper). One school of thought argues that papers are still too cheap – when *The Guardian* put its price up a third in 1974, it pointed out that British Rail coffee was still more expensive – both in comparison to other things, and because the cheapness makes some of them too dependent on advertising for plugging the gap between what the readers pay and what the papers cost. The other school argues that the cheapness of papers explained their deep and wide penetration in Britain compared with other countries, and that this precious asset, for democracy, and for the advertisers, should be preserved as far as newspaper economics allow.

There is little doubt that superinflation and decimalization have destroyed the concept of the 'right' price for anything. Do the buyers of *The Sunday Times* at 15p realize they are paying three old shillings? Does a rise of 3p, which is what the entire paper used to cost, deter buyers anymore? It is too soon to say; the initial reaction by the public to the spate of price rises in 1974 did not seem to be to cancel the papers. But relative to other things, newspapers have risen substantially in price, and there is a danger that at some point, each price rise will make more readers defect. The most eloquent newspaper marketing guru, Harry Henry, who helped plan Thomson's introduction of the colour magazine to Britain, has contested crude suggestions that newspapers raise their prices to a level sufficient to displace the importance of advertising as a source of revenue.

The total market for newspaper sales as it currently exists is the market at a particular level of prices . . . newspapers at their present level of total circulation are neither a necessity of life nor an addictive drug, so that the total market cannot be regarded as likely to be immune from any major increase in the level of selling prices: there is the permanent possibility (even without price increases) of the substitution by the public of other sources of information supply, particularly television, while advertisers already have alternative forms of commercial communication to which they can turn should the coverage provided by the national press diminish to any material extent.[15]

But the newspaper market is not such a pure exercise in competition as all that. Beaverbrook deliberately held the price of the *Express* low in 1947 to persecute the Labour 'Govt. Press'.

Refuse to increase your selling price, tighten your belt and let the suffering and misery descend upon the wretches who supported the Socialists in the last election.[16]

Was this the voice of non-economic man, or just the instinctive monopolist?

One reason for the growth in the size of newspapers is that managements have had to provide more space for surveys and for advertisements in the body of the paper. The physical impact of rising break-even costs is that newspapers have to be fatter to accommodate the advertising they need to meet such costs. Logically, this process can continue. In practice, production and distribution problems will tend to set a limit. As a result, under existing market pressures and in the absence of any corrective, rising costs are driving newspapers upmarket so as to get more advertising revenue for a given cost structure. In 1973 the *Financial Times* got 80 per cent of its revenue from advertising and *The Times* 73 per cent (table 3.1, page 44).

While the upmarket march may be a sensible policy for one or two newspapers, it cannot work for too many. Although the advertising market can support, with varying degrees of security, the existing quality newspapers, the position of all newspapers cannot be improved unless the total amount of advertising revenue is increased. The chase for higher revenue may come to a sticky end.

It is for this reason that newspapers will be forced, sooner or later, to look at the cost side of the profit and loss account. This means lower manning levels, a shallower differential between the wages of both journalist and production workers relative to workers in other industries, new working methods and the introduction of new typesetting and composing technology. It is only after all this has been tried that people will believe that the crises of the newspaper industry are not all of its own making.

References

1 *Costs and Revenues of National Newspapers*, National Board for Prices and Incomes, Report No. 141 (Cmnd. 4277), February 1970.
2 STEED, Wickham, *The Press*, Penguin Books, 1938, p. 144.
3 Royal Commission on the Press, 1961–1962, Documentary evidence, Volume 1, p. 102.
4 *Ibid*, p. 141.
5 KING, Cecil, *The Future of the Press*, MacGibbon and Kee, 1967.
6 As note 3, p. 151.
7 Royal Commission on the Press, 1947–1949, Q 8656 and Q 8660.
8 TAYLOR, A. J. P., *Beaverbrook*, Hamish Hamilton, 1972; Penguin Books, 1974, p. 854.
9 *Ibid*, p. 805.

10 *Ibid*, p. 277.
11 *Ibid*, p. 489.
12 CURRAN, J., 'The Impact of Television on the Audience for National Newspapers 1945–1968,' *Media Sociology*, edited by Jeremy Turnstall, Constable, 1970.
13 JONES, D. A. N. 'What's News?' in *The Press We Deserve*, edited by Richard Boston, Routledge and Kegan Paul, 1970, p. 32.
14 *The Guardian*, 28 August 1974, p. 15.
15 HENRY, Harry, *Perspectives in Management, Marketing and Research*, Crosby Lockwood and Son, 1971, page 171.
16 As note 8, p. 747.

5 The press on the budgets

'It is absolutely right that Conservative Governments should produce Conservative budgets and Labour Governments Socialist ones.' ('A radical Tory budget,' *The Times*, 21 March 1971)

'Are the tax reforms worth the effort? The Finance Bill, with its clear implication that the government is wedded to its doctrinaire ideas and intends to give no concession to hard cases, gives a negative answer.' ('Is it worth it?', *The Times*, 28 April 1965)

This chapter* draws on a systematic analysis of the reception given by the quality press to budgets between 1964 and 1973. The aim of the analysis was to test the hypothesis that such comment fell within a fairly narrow band, a band that shifted over time, but one markedly narrower than that extending over the whole political and academic spectrum.

The analysis bore out the initial hypothesis partially but not fully. The notion of a band well within the political extremes was broadly confirmed; and, as discussed in Chapter One, the width of the band was significant – the ideological distance from *The Daily Telegraph* to *The Guardian* is substantial. There was nonetheless considerable concentration of views and of the main focus of papers' attention; some tendency – though only modest in strength – for opinions to move together over time; and some slight evidence of a double standard – Conservative governments

* This chapter draws largely on work by Jeremy Andrews.

being expected to implement their philosophy and Labour governments being advised to put theirs on the back burner.

Newspapers almost certainly influence the public much more by their presentation of news and news analysis than by the opinions expressed in their leading articles. But our central object here has been to reflect newspapers' own concerns and ideological positions. Analysis of leading articles seemed the most practicable indication of these.

What newspapers say or do not say about budgets reveals their position on the redistribution of income. This was an issue that until the early 1970s had lain half-buried under the assumption that economic growth would satisfy the demands that lay behind the ancient call of the poorer groups for fair shares. Everyone would have more, so that quarrels about the division of the cake could be left aside. The main preoccupation of the leader writers of the quality papers in the decade from 1964 to 1973 was with economic management – with the effects of the budget on growth, inflation, and the balance of payments and unemployment. Their prescriptions differed after the fashions of the time, though with the exception of *The Observer* and a few elliptic asides, they were unanimous in not discussing the desirability or possibility of devaluation in the first three years of the period.

This is a striking example of the importance of the selection of the questions that the press discusses, and does not discuss. It is admittedly fair comment that in focusing on economic growth and economic management – and also in rejecting use of the exchange rate as an instrument of management – the press was merely following the lead of the leadership of the major parties, including the Labour party under the inaugural Wilson attempt to shed ideological divisions. But that is precisely our complaint. The press, led by the quality press, did not form an independent body of criticism. It did not draw, as it could have done, on work being done at least peripherally in the universities indicating the limitations of economic growth in solving the problems of the worst off. Significantly, this work – e.g., by Professor Richard Titmuss and his school on the problems of the poorest and by Professor James Meade on the cumulative processes of economic inequality, all published in the first half of the 1960s – had to be rediscovered by the quality press ten years later when the political tide had turned. At the relevant time, the press was so anxious to welcome the new political consensus that it took aboard even such fatuities as Mr Wilson's 'socialism is science' doctrine. The press did not act as a check on the instincts, rationalizations and self-delusions of Britain's all party establishment. It reinforced them.

The redistribution of income means that income is taken from some and given to others, obviously one of the fundamental issues of politics. But the redistributive effects of changes in the tax structure were often discussed in the newspapers in a way that sounded politically neutral. The criteria were the apparently non-ideological ones of whether the measures would be 'practical', whether they would help those 'in need', and whether they would detract from the operation of 'incentives', which were conventionally and curiously assumed to influence work habits only of businessmen and managers. For whatever reason, most of the quality press came out against government measures that would put a higher tax burden on the AB readers, whom they valued the most. The *Daily Telegraph* and *Sunday Telegraph* did so most stridently, the *Financial Times* most sensibly, *The Times* most long-windedly, *The Sunday Times* most confusedly. With the frequent exception of *The Guardian* and occasional exception of *The Observer*, leaders stuck close to the conservative centre.

In general the quality press opposed the changes in direct taxation made by the Wilson government that took office in 1964, encouraged and welcomed the decision to deflate by using indirect taxes after the devaluation of 1967, and gave a warm welcome to the stand-on-your-own-two-feet policies of the first phase of the Heath government that was elected in 1970; broadly, it was against high marginal rates of personal tax, at the top, unmindful of increases in marginal rates at the bottom of the scale, in favour of lower corporation taxes, against additional welfare spending and social service benefits when, as in 1964, improving them required the raising of extra revenue.

James Callaghan's mini-budget in November 1964 raised

pensions, with only part of the extra expense to be covered by increased National Insurance contributions. At the same time petrol duty was raised by 6d a gallon, and income tax by 6d in the pound. While it was intended that the extra taxation be mildly deflationary, its main purpose was to finance the pensions increase. *The Times* did not approve.

Social justice, if it is to mean anything in this context means relating income to need; and, to put it at its bluntest, this is not likely to be achieved by the crude disbursement of lump sums in all directions . . . The only guiding principle in the Chancellor's proposals, it must be suspected, is that extra benefits cannot be handed out on this scale without doing some good somewhere.
(*'More of the same all round'*, 12 November 1964)

The Guardian welcomed the higher pensions as 'sorely needed' but elsewhere the increase was treated as an unnecessary diversion. This was the characteristic reaction of the *Financial Times* in a rare reference to the anathema of the exchange rate.

There is no doubt that if Labour had been really serious about improving the balance of payments, it would have paid more attention to exports – even to the point of reconsidering the exchange parity – and less to an immediate increase in social benefits.
(*'The Economy after the Budget'*, 13 November 1964)

In similar vein the *Financial Times* chided Callaghan for misdirecting his energies in April 1965 when he introduced two new taxes, corporation tax at 40 per cent, and capital gains tax at 30 per cent.

It is to be hoped that . . . Mr Callaghan has not cancelled out the moderate effect of his Budget with the more extreme nature of his ideas about tax reform. If it had been less 'wide-ranging' and were concerned to stimulate exports, investment and saving, its impact would have been more forceful.
(*'Good in outline, bad in parts'*, 7 April 1965)

The Times made the point more emphatically.

When Britain still faces the need to pay off vast foreign debts, is this the

best way to use the nation's time? Are the tax reforms worth the effort? The Finance Bill with its clear implication that the government is wedded to its doctrinaire ideas and intends to give no concessions to hard cases, gives a negative answer.
('*Is it worth it?*, 28 April 1965)

An explanation for the Chancellor's behaviour was given by the *Telegraph*.

As was doubtless to be expected [Mr Callaghan] felt impelled to gild the pill of the higher drink and tobacco taxes by gratifying his supporters' emotions – and possibly his own – in the most obvious ways: that is to say, by harrying the higher-paid business and professional men and by harrying capital by various measures.
('*Socialist answer*', 7 April 1965)

The *Financial Times* thought:

the extension of short term gains to twelve months, the charging of the long term tax at the high rate of 30 per cent and the refusal to allow entertainment as a charge against tax all suggest that the Government is ready to go a long way to meet trade union prejudices in order to win cooperation in an incomes policy.
('*First reactions to the Budget*', 10 April 1965)

but *The Guardian* concentrated on the ideological point that:

the Labour Government is also taking a large stride towards bringing about a fairer distribution of incomes – and of tax burdens ... The capital gains tax, abolition of the surtax concession on covenants, the attack on business expenses – these are all measures that in the long run must make for greater equality. Mr Callaghan has yet to make a real assault on accumulated wealth. For this radical reform of our antiquated system of death duties (now almost wholly ineffective) would be needed.
('*The strategy of a Labour Budget*', 7 April 1965)

The Observer also guardedly welcomed this early version of the social contract:

Politically the Budget has certainly made it easier for Mr Brown to persuade the unions to accept the principle of an incomes policy by

introducing a capital gains tax and attacking business expenses. Indeed, quite apart from these tactical considerations, there is probably a case for reversing the trend towards greater inequalities in wealth.
(*'The one-legged men'*, 11 April 1965)

It was following this budget that *The Times* published a leader entitled *'Overtaxation?'* presenting some of the arguments often used by the quality press against high marginal rates of direct taxation which concluded:

It may well be that the scope now left for increasing this [economic] welfare by means of trying to redistribute income between large groups is limited . . . In this kind of situation the introduction of new flat rate taxes with few exceptions is likely to create many hard cases.
(20 April 1965)

In other words, there are socially acceptable limits to redistribution; readers of the quality press in the subsequent five years might have been forgiven for gaining the impression that 'hardship' was a condition suffered exclusively by surtax payers. One of the July 1966 measures that were intended to avert devaluation was a 10 per cent surcharge on surtax. *The Times* was particularly upset by the Government's priorities.

Again it is a gratuitous provocation and a great disincentive. . . . The amount to be collected is derisory. Many surtax payers nowadays are key executives on whom Britain's industrial future specially depends. This tax class is singled out compared with all other income earners for discriminatory treatment. The proposal seems nothing less than a primitive kind of class legislation designed to appease an uncomfortable left wing.
(*'A stiffish dose at last'*, 21 July 1966)

The Times knew where it would have preferred the measures to bite – 'It is a pity that the social services appear to have escaped almost unscathed.' And the *Telegraph* was less restrained.

They should understand now if they did not know before that by 'social justice' Mr Wilson means the selective persecution of the middle class . . . The spirit in which [the package] is brought forward is one of

undiminished arrogance and class spite . . . How long will it take the British people to learn that such measures as those just announced are not the peculiar products of crisis? They are what Socialism is all about.
(*'Deflating Socialism'*, 21 July 1966)

When a socialist Chancellor could bring himself to use indirect taxation to reduce consumption, as did Jenkins in the budget of March 1968, he was congratulated by the *Financial Times*, and by *The Times*, which hopefully saw in the decision not to raise direct taxes 'a defence of the incentives that now exist', but he was not congratulated by *The Guardian*.

The decision to leave income tax unchanged, however, involves a further element of regression in the pattern of the total tax burden. Overall the increases will fall more lightly the higher up one is in the wealth and income scale. This must be a disappointment to those who expect a Labour Government to use taxation as a means to narrow the differentials in wealth and income in British society.
(*'A Banker's Budget: higher costs all round'*, 20 March 1968)

The Guardian had a few months earlier fiercely objected to the way the Government had set about reducing its expenditure.

Some of the economies – the restoration of prescription charges in particular – are nothing more than an abject genuflection before the anti-welfare prejudices of the gnomes and bankers to whom we are indebted.
(*'A mixed bag of cuts – but where is the strategy?'*, 17 January 1968)

This did not imply that *The Guardian* had turned against bankers and the industry they finance. Quite the opposite: drawing on its Manchester liberal tradition, it had a strong belief in a lively private sector, and consistently supported lower corporation taxes. For example,

The best sort of expansion would be one brought about by a revival of investment in manufacturing industry. A cut in corporation tax would help, if it were politically possible. (Profits have been squeezed hard in the past year.)
(*'A budget this year for 1968'*, 7 April 1967)

And this was the line it mostly stuck to, though when corporation tax was raised by 2½ per cent in the 1969 budget, *The Guardian* reckoned that:

If industrialists really feel that we are at last returning to a policy of sustained growth they may not allow their enthusiasm for modernised plant and machinery to be dampened by having to pay extra corporation tax.
('*A moderate budget*', 16 April 1969)

But *The Times* objected to the budget partly because tax relief was disallowed on bank interest. This was a blow to those with high incomes who wanted to accumulate capital; the technique was to borrow heavily and buy shares or property with the proceeds. The interest on the loan could be deducted from income, thus reducing the personal tax bill, and the loan would eventually be paid off from the profits on the assets acquired – profits which were taxed at capital gains tax rates of 30 per cent rather than at the much higher income tax rates. *The Times* Business News looked at the phenomenon the other way round.

The fact . . . that a man earning £20 000 a year pays an effective interest rate of less than one per cent a year is simply a reflection of the extraordinarily high rates of surtax. The remedy is to lower the high rates of tax on larger earned incomes.
('*Illogicality of new tax policy*', 17 April 1969)

Which is what the Conservatives did when they got back in power. In October 1970 the Chancellor of the Exchequer, Anthony Barber, had a mini-budget which proposed a cut of 2½ per cent in both corporation and income tax. Although his supporters had to wait eighteen months before the tax relief on borrowed money was reinstated, they were delighted with what they had been given. The *Telegraph*, by far the most partisan in its editorial comment, explained the rationale of the new Tory leaders in almost liturgical style.

Reducing the power of the State and the weight of taxation, as with certain of Mr Heath's other policies like the reform of our chaotic industrial relations, is an enormous act of faith. No one can possibly prove in advance that the British will work harder if they are allowed to keep more of the fruits of their toil . . . But . . . it is surely common sense that a much more competitive environment in Britain will stimulate a correspondingly higher economic growth rate. If we achieve that, all else will be given unto us – including a buoyant revenue for the Exchequer.

(*'Barber's act of faith'*, 29 October 1970)

The Times was scarcely less enthusiastic when the first full budget of the new administration was announced.

What is certain about this budget, and very good, is its political impact. It is a radical budget in that it meets problems directly and tries to deal with them completely . . . This is also a clearly Conservative budget, and is the first such budget for many years. It is absolutely right that Conservative Governments should produce Conservative budgets and Labour Governments Socialist ones; democracy is served by choice as well as by compromise. Most of the budgets of the past Conservative administration have made no attempt to change the fiscal consensus as it had been left by the war and by the Attlee Government. They generally accepted the high priority given to equalising society as against making it dynamic. They assumed an underlying hostility to private wealth was normal . . . they were ashamed of private capital . . . Mr Barber is plainly convinced that a capitalist system will only work if it accepts its own logic, if it encourages the development and investment of capital and the earning and retention of high incomes . . . This will, of course, be attacked on social grounds, though there is a stronger case than many think for creating a society with strong rewards for success.

(*'A radical Tory budget'*, 31 March 1971)

This was a budget in which the burden of income taxes on the rich was greatly reduced, and in which many loopholes blocked by the previous administration were reopened. The *Financial Times* felt:

The lowering of the top rate and the taxation at the earned rate of the first slice of unearned income may be opposed by Labour but are plainly justified. . . . On the other hand, the concession to large surtax payers, the abolition of short-term gains tax, the change in estate duty provisions and the disaggregation of wives' and children's income will help

both to restore a sense of incentive and to reduce the amount of time at present consumed in tax avoidance.
(*'Something for everyone'*, 31 March 1971)

The image of businessmen thus fostered is of a hard-working corps of entrepreneurs and executives distracted from getting on with the job by the necessity of spending hours with the tax accountants, which is precisely how the *Telegraph* had seen them in 1964.

The 6d on the standard rate of income tax bears most heavily on the professional and higher 'executive' groups, including the export managers who may now spend more mental energy on adjusting their private budgets and less on selling exports.
(*'A little stop'*, 12 November 1964)

The Observer took a more sceptical view of what made people spend their mental energy.

Are the present tax levels really a disincentive to effort? No one knows. Contrary to popular belief, Britain is not a particularly high taxed country (although there is plenty of scope for improving the tax *system* – a different matter altogether). Again there is no evidence to show that Britain's comparatively slow economic growth is caused by our tax rates; plenty of other equally likely explanations are available.
(*'The new Toryism'*, 1 November 1970)

The Sunday Times had some general reservations but thought:

criticism of the Government's plans will be more fruitful if it focuses on the method rather than the principle. To impose and increase user charges, related to income, for housing, education, and the health service may be some way from a welfare utopia. But those who object to it must say how otherwise they would build more schools and hospitals . . . Differential council-house rents are a just objective and the Government should press on with their intention to subsidise needy private tenants as well.
(*'The plan without a strategy'*, 1 November 1970)

Very pragmatic.

It was left to *The Guardian* to question the reasoning that lay behind the Tory philosophy, mark I, which saw an incentive effect from tax giveaways to the higher income groups but was blind to any disincentive effect from increased marginal tax rates, or more selective welfare benefits, for the lower income groups.

Working class people in general come badly out of the budget. The reduction in income tax this year for a married man with two children earning £1,456 a year or £28 a week (the national average) will be £43. The reduction for a married man with two children earning £5 000 a year will be £130. This may be what the Government means by an incentive system. But its effect on trade union negotiators will be to make them ask for more, not less. Widening the gap between rich and poor does not help to control wage inflation.

('*Mr Barber gambles on a Tory road to growth*', 31 March 1971)

The Guardian was also sceptical about the theory of making the beneficiaries pay more for the social services both on the same grounds that the cost of paying for what had been free would exacerbate the push for higher wages but also:

[Selective school meal charges] will mean that more children will realise while they are still at school that society is divided, and that they belong to the unenvied part of it. This does not help the British to become One Nation.

('*The cost of Mr Barber*', 28 October 1970)

The Guardian appears radical only by comparison with the other papers. Its soul is in the middle of the road, waving at the traffic coming from the right to move over to the centre, and flagging down the traffic from the left to tell it not to go so fast. A few months after reminding the Conservatives about the nation on the other side of the road, it is back to the old theme that the trouble with budgets helping the well-off is that, justified though this may be, it makes the trade unions stroppy.

Labour governments have a tendency to be so obsessed with the need for equity that they neglect the incentive which is an essential part of the drive to growth. The Conservatives this year have paid too much attention to the reasonably well-off people who voted for them, and who

expected a lot after six years of socialism. That, too, can be counter-productive, for a stable expansion also depends on sensible restraint by trade unions, and a fair budget is a factor in that.
('*What Mr Heath left out*', 5 April 1971)

While many will agree with *The Observer* that selectivity 'is an excellent principle', because only those who are needy get help, the introduction of greater selectivity at a time when the better off were getting indiscriminate handouts helped create an atmosphere of divisiveness, as well as high implicit marginal tax rates. Few saw this at the time. The quality newspapers had got what they were after. Although not unremittingly critical of social spending and higher pensions and family allowances (after the somewhat ill-tempered outburst in 1964), they had hammered home the necessity for greater selectivity. The *Financial Times* argued the case for relating welfare benefits more closely to the income of the recipient in 1968.

Some action on this front is imperative, not merely to demonstrate the Government's readiness to treat the economic situation seriously but because this is where fairly large and immediate savings in public expenditure can be made without causing undue hardship. Prescriptions can be charged and a higher charge made for school meals while exempting those in greatest need.

The policy had wide scope for application since £100 million

could eventually be saved by pressing local authorities more vigorously to charge economic rents to tenants who can afford them.
('*Where the axe should fall*', 15 January 1968)

These suggestions bore fruit in the Selsdon Park strategy, named after the hotel in Croydon where Heath and his band decided to adopt a robust brand of Toryism; the proposals were incorporated in Barber's early budgets to an enthusiastic reception by most of the quality press. Not all the papers were as zealous as the *Telegraph*.

Doubts about Mr Barber's mini-budget must centre largely, indeed, on whether it does enough . . . There are, for instance, still big savings to

be made in the largely indiscriminate welfare services. We are told, it is true, that there will eventually be savings of up to £200 million a year from a revamping of housing subsidies.
(*'Barber's bonus'*, 28 October 1970)

But *The Times* was nonetheless pleased.

The Government must be absolved from any charge of butchery. What they have done is to transfer some of the responsibility for paying for the social services. . . . Given all the fuss over deciding who should be exempt from paying when the Labour Government restored prescription charges in 1968, it is understandable that this Government should want to get rather more money out of those who can afford to pay. Consequently, there can be no objection in principle to the proposal for raising charges in due course to a proportion of the cost of the individual prescription – up to a ceiling that has not as yet been specified . . . The case for moderate social service charges has been argued in these columns before . . . In general this part of the Government's package seems all right.
(*'No attack on welfare'*, 28 October 1970)

However, *The Times* felt that the Government ought to give 'careful second thoughts' to the new and selective Family Income Supplement – and to the changes in housing subsidies because of administrative difficulties and the possible 'disincentive' effects of the measures. This advice was given somewhat late in the day in view of the effect of its earlier, contrary appeals. Though the paper was not wholeheartedly penitent, it continued to claim that selectivity in the social services was a goal worth pursuing.

If only *The Times* had appraised policies of which it approved with the same incisive criticism it applied to those which it opposed. Then perhaps it would have asked in 1970 whether tax reforms were worth the effort, and would perhaps have concluded that 'the clear implication that the Government is wedded to its doctrinaire ideas, and intends to give no concession to hard cases, gives a negative answer', as it did in 1965. Similarly, the *Financial Times* might then have pointed out that the Government was ready to go a long way to meet City prejudices as it had in 1965 frowned on the way the Wilson government went to meet trade union prejudices. The *Telegraph* might have wondered if Barber

D

was gratifying his supporters' emotions – and possibly his own – by harrying the low paid and welfare claimants by various measures, as it had wondered about Callaghan in 1965.

As the most detached of the quality newspapers from the audience to which the other quality newspapers successfully appeal, *The Guardian* accepted with better grace than *The Times*, whose phrase it was, that just as Conservative governments introduce conservative budgets, Labour governments will introduce socialist ones.

The Conservative party is the businessman's party, and it was only to be expected that there would be concessions to the rich. There are big ones; but it is at least fair to say that the biggest proportionate benefits go to those with a modest capital, and there is not much for the ultra-rich . . . It might have been worse.

('*The Budget: big and bold, but partly defective*', 22 March 1972)

Tolerance can be a great virtue, even an exotic quality, in Fleet Street, and *The Guardian*'s restraint in its criticism cannot be faulted in itself. But no parallel understanding of the implementation of Labour ideology emerges from the *Telegraph* – or from *The Times* for that matter. Against the vociferous pressure from the rest of the upmarket press, the lone and muted voice of dissent hardly constitutes a balance of editorial opinion.

6 The press in Europe

'Le système economique dans lequel vit ou survit la presse reste fondé sur le profit: il pousse à la concentration en meme temps qu'à la facilité.'

(The press lives – survives, rather – in an economic system that remains founded on profit: this leads to the concentration of ownership, and to superficiality.)

Le Monde, 31 October 1974

The press is financially precarious in other European countries besides Britain. Rapid cost and wage inflation, and the doubling of newsprint prices between 1972 and 1974, have added to its longer standing problems. Broadly, the circulations of 'popular'-type (the strict distinction applies only in Britain) newspapers are in decline because of the pull of television, unless like Britain's *Sun* and Germany's *Bild Zeitung* they have an added dose of sex. Newspapers that have overt connexions with political parties have suffered a loss of readership or, like the Gaullist *La Nation*, have folded. Many 'quality'-type newspapers have seen their readership, if not their profits, grow. There is a continuing trend towards highly profitable local monopolies in the non-national press. A brief examination of the press in a number of European countries shows that government indirect aid is widespread and that newspapers are swallowing their pride and reluctance and are beginning to ask for more.

When it comes to working out a policy for newspapers, governments tend to call forth commissions. Britain was not alone in having one in 1974. Sweden's press was being examined by a commission, like Britain's the third since the war. The Dutch government was working on a long-awaited plan for all the media. The German government had an inquiry. And a parliamentary commission in Italy was set up to make recommendations for a new law to subsidize newspapers. The existing aids in continental Europe mostly give a generalized and indirect subsidy to all newspapers, without trying to achieve much more.

Sweden has the most interventionist approach to newspapers. This is partly because of the role that newspapers play in the party political system, partly because the Swedes are great believers in social engineering, and partly because they are assiduous newspaper readers: fifty-five adult Swedes out of a hundred buy a newspaper every day, compared with forty-nine out of a hundred in Britain. In the 1920s there were over 200 independent publications, but the decline set in after 1950 and in the following fifteen years, eighty titles ceased publication. As in other countries, the pattern was for the leading paper in each region to get stronger and to draw advertising from its rivals, thereby making them physically smaller and financially weaker. The growth element has been evening newspapers, and two Stockholm papers, *Expressen* with a circulation over 600 000 and *Aftonbladet* with over 500 000, have achieved national distribution. With the big Stockholm morning daily *Dagens Nyheter*, and the *Svenska Dagbladet*, the organ of industry and the conservatives, they are Sweden's only real national press. They are an odd mixture of the sensational and the serious, combining most features of *The Times*, the *News of the World* and the *Daily Express*.

Party political debate in Sweden is conducted largely through newspapers and most of them are tied to parties. Except, ironically, where there is a local monopoly, and to reach the whole market the paper has adopted a much more neutral tone. For this special reason the trend to monopoly became a matter of greater concern to politicians than it has been in Britain. The statistics showing the division of circulation between the parties began to look more and more unbalanced. The Social Democrat papers, and those of the second largest party, the Centre Party, were typically the ones losing circulation and playing second fiddle to the non-socialist papers. The first press commission in 1963 recommended that aid be doled out to papers via the parties. Instead the parties themselves were given state funds to spend on newspapers or on other forms of propaganda as they pleased and about £1 million a year is spent on newspapers by the parties. When the main Social Democrat organ, the *Stockholms-Tidningen*, folded in 1966, another press commission was set up, which made some recommendations that were adopted. On its recommendations a fund was set up to lend money to 'secondary papers' – the paper or papers that trailed behind the leading paper in each circulation region. A sum of £2½ million a year is available for loans to finance investment in plant or machinery or in anything that will improve the position of such papers. Only those papers that are too weak to borrow at commercial rates are eligible. They pay no interest for three years, and then a rate about 4 per cent below market rates. Another £2½ million is handed out to reduce the costs of distributing newspapers. In each region, the papers had an arrangement with a co-operative distribution organization, the press bureau, but the weaker newspapers paid more per copy than the strong ones. If the papers in each region agree to pay the same, they get a distribution discount of 0·3p per copy. It is a voluntary scheme but most papers have joined it. In addition the post office bears a loss of £3 million a year for delivering newspapers and since postal distribution is important this is another useful aid.

In 1971 a further subsidy was introduced: a grant relating to usage of newsprint, of £750 per tonne in 1974 when the cost was over £150 per tonne – with a maximum of £1 million for any single paper. The subsidy is payable only for the newsprint used for editorial matter, and for papers whose advertising space was under half the total. Again it is designed primarily for secondary papers, although in special circumstances leading newspapers are given it as well.

In addition the Swedish government spends over £1 million on placing advertisements in the newspapers and magazines to give the public more information about civic affairs; the government finances two schools of journalism; and newspapers are exempt from Value Added Tax, which means that the newspaper buyers are spared some £15 million a year they would otherwise have to fork out. In all, total indirect and direct government aid amounted in 1974 to £35 million, including the loans. This is financed by a tax of 6 per cent on newspaper advertising (which brings in about £3½ million) and a 10 per cent tax on all other advertising; thus, to some extent, rich newspapers subsidize poorer ones. This tax has been criticized, by the Social Democrats and left-wing parties among others, on the grounds that it has reduced the level of advertising expenditure, especially in times when the economy is not doing well. The third press commission will have to judge whether this has been so.

The civilized system under which the largest opposition papers, the Conservative *Svenska Dagbladet* and the Liberal *Göteborgs Handelstidning* were among those getting the heaviest government grants was, in fact, far from ideal. The subsidy did not keep the latter paper alive; it folded in September 1973. And, according to some observers, there has been some emasculation in the subsidized press. Since the *Svenska Dagbladet* is a second newspaper in the Stockholm region, it is subsidized at the expense of the *Dagens Nyheter*, the biggest morning newspaper in Sweden. But it does not seem to attack the Social Democratic government, its supposed political enemy, in the way it once did.

Clearly, an undesirably narrow consensus band of opinion can emerge when the state pays the piper, just as it can when, as in Britain, the need to attract an affluent readership calls the tune. To some extent, Sweden's narrow band can be explained by a strong social pressure to conform, illustrated by the following incident. At the height of the Vietnam war, when the Swedish press was a chorus of disapproval of American policy, the managing director of a conservative chain of newspapers approached the correspondent of a British newspaper and suggested that he write a story saying that not all Swedes were anti-American; many of the readers had relatives there, and influential subscribers and advertisers were worried that the campaign would affect their exports. When asked why his papers could not write the story, the director said that if an editor departed too far from the prevalent consensus, he would be attacked by the government and by his readers, but that something that had first appeared abroad could be legitimately reprinted. The same group used to send out pre-cooked leaders to all its newspapers every day: since all of them held – or were held to – the same principles, it was regarded as a needless waste of energy to get twenty journalists to write twenty leaders. But for all the faults of the Swedish subsidy scheme, it does encourage a certain diversity of newspapers and prevents a wholesale movement to the right that would occur if market forces operated unchecked.

Market forces have certainly not operated unchecked in Italy. If they had, most newspapers would have had to shut down, since the Italian press is thought to have made a loss of £32 million in 1973, and almost the same again in 1974. Italian newspapers are subsidized by their owners, and the result is editorial dependence, and a style of writing aimed at the newspapers' backers rather than readers. This partly accounts for the low newspaper readership in Italy: only about one person in eight buys a paper.

There is neither a national nor a popular press as in Britain. There are newspapers with national circulations and those with local circulations, but there is very little difference in format between the two. There are only two newspapers that can be considered national: *Corriere della Sera* (of Milan, with a daily print order of 600 000 – there are no reliable circulation figures and the print order figures must be treated with caution) and *La Stampa* (Turin, 500 000). Each carries two pages of local news, and local papers carry international and economic news. The third largest paper is *Il Messaggero* (Rome, 300 000 plus) which, typically, changed ownership twice in the year to mid-1974. There are seventeen other papers with a print order over 100 000, including three sports papers and the communist daily, *L'Unità*. These twenty account for 70 per cent of all daily newspapers. The place of popular dailies is taken by popular glossy weeklies, such as *Oggi*. The serious press is buttressed by the weekly *L'Espresso*, which in its new news magazine format maintains its remarkable and effective combination of radical political comment, informed business comment, and a minimum of one nude a week in its cultural section.

A great handicap for the Italian press is that newspapers are one of the items in the shopping basket which makes up the index to which almost all labour contracts are pegged. A 10 lire rise in the price of newspapers equals a 0·42 per cent rise in the index, which in turn leads to an increase in wages of something like £20 million a year. From December 1973 to June 1974, after fierce battles with the government, the price of newspapers went up in two stages from 90 lire to 150 lire, more than a cup of espresso coffee. This still did not wipe out the deficit for the year. Price control has deterred new investment, even though newspapers qualify for a scheme that gives subsidized interest rates on loans for technological improvements.

A further handicap is a complicated levy-subsidy scheme for paper. To promote the domestic paper industry, newspapers have to buy home-made newsprint, and all paper users have to pay a surcharge on paper to a state body. This body, together with the state itself, then pays out a subsidy to newsprint users, which varies inversely with the amount they use; the more they use, the less the subsidy. But it only amounted to £5 million in 1973. Newspaper publishers also get a share of television advertising. A government commission decides what the share is to be and can increase television's share only if newspaper advertising goes up. The subsidies do not create either a free or a healthy press. A new law is awaited without much optimism.

The extinction of profit has driven newspapers into the arms of big business enterprises, state and private. They can absorb the losses of the paper into their own often sizeable losses and use the newspapers to plead for whatever favours they want from politicians. Control by industrialists has been steadily tightening. In 1973 the Crespi family, one of the last of Italy's press families, sold control of *Corriere della Sera* to one group controlled by Gianni Agnelli, the head of Fiat, and to Angelo Moratti, an oil baron. Agnelli already controlled *La Stampa*, based in Turin with his car factories, and thus had an influence over the largest and most respected dailies in Italy. But in 1974, to the surprise of its staff, control of *Corriere della Sera* changed yet again. Rizzoli, the publishing group, bought it with money that everyone believed to have been supplied by Montedison, the huge textile and chemical group run by Eugenio Cefis. This left Agnelli controlling one of the papers, and Cefis in control of the other. Cefis had recently also bought Turin's other newspaper, which had been vociferously anti-Fiat. Cefis closed down *La Gazzetta del Popolo*, presumably as a return favour to Agnelli – though the journalists rebelled against the closure and managed to continue to bring the paper out.

Although figures and details of ownership are rarely divulged officially, Montedison is believed to have paid £20 million for *Corriere della Sera*, which was then making a loss of £5 million. This was on top of another large sum that Cefis had spent on gaining control of *Il Messaggero*, of the right-wing *Il Tempo* (Rome, 262 000), *Il Resto del Carlino* (Bologna, 258 000). He has also backed a new paper, *Il Giornale* (Milan, 150 000), which has set out to be a journalist cooperative, on the lines of *Le Monde*. In the first few months following the purchases, the newspapers had not shown undue deference to their new master; but it is unlikely that Cefis would spend up to £50 million out of altruism.

The state energy corporation ENI controls *Il Giorno* (Milan, 300 000), which is a fairly objective paper except when the subject is energy; it did not mention the country's 1974 petrol scandals. Together, the private groups, Fiat, Montedison and Monti (an oil company), and sundry state enterprises, control the newspapers whose circulation account for about half the daily total in the country. For the rest, there are eight papers which follow a political party line, such as the Socialist *Avanti* or the Christian Democrat *Il Popolo* and there are a host of papers owned directly by political parties, an assorted variety of groups like banks, farmers' associations, or minor industrialists. The only saving grace is that there are a lot of different newspaper string-pullers – or were until the industrialists moved in.

Italian journalists have taken a long time to rouse themselves to criticize the system. This is because journalism is a grossly over-protected profession, with very high rates of pay, an excellent health insurance scheme (worth its weight in gold in a country where there is no national health system), security of tenure, housing cooperatives and pensions which pay about 80 per cent of final salary. Journalists have begun to seek some democracy within newspapers; they have asked for effective measures to prevent concentration of newspaper ownership; they want the balance sheets of newspapers to be published; and they want more subsidies and credit for modernization. But with a serious economic crisis in 1974, demands for the reform of the press fell by the wayside.

The press in France has no strong tradition of independence from government or private business. But it has shown itself anxious, if not determined, to keep as far away from government as its finances will allow. The ruthless interference of the French government into the affairs of the state-owned radio and television service, which has somewhat diminished under the liberalizing influence of President Giscard d'Estaing, stands as an object lesson of what could happen. The worst that the press has had to put up with in the past is the confiscation of an entire edition that displeased the government.

The press gets indirect help, and would like more. The most valuable support is the reduced postal tariff, which is of most benefit to the many weeklies and periodicals. This is worth about £67 million a year, and there are other concessions on rail freight rates, and on telephone and telegram rates. French journalists also get a generous tax allowance to cover expenses, although this may be stopped as they also get cash amounts from their newspapers to cover them. The other important concession is the exemption – common in most of Europe – from Value Added Tax, which saves the consumer £20 million a year on purchase of his papers. A bone of contention between the press and the government is that VAT can be recouped only to the extent that it is charged. Newspapers charge VAT on their advertising and can thus offset only the VAT they have paid to an equivalent amount. This bears hard on the papers with the least advertising, as does another measure, the payment of a salary tax on VAT-exempted revenue.

The rise in the cost of newspaper production has taken its toll of newspapers. A small ad hoc subsidy of £$\frac{1}{2}$ million paid in 1973 to papers with a circulation of under 200 000 did not prevent the closure in 1974 of *Combat*, the old resistance paper, and of *La Nation*. All newspapers felt the squeeze, which was worsened by tight government control of cover prices. But what to do? At the end of a long series of articles in November 1974 on the press in Europe – '*Journaux en péril*' – *Le Monde* was rather depressed about the prospects. For France it suggested a round table conference, in which editors, journalists, printing workers and representatives of the government would get together and draft a statute setting out the various government measures that could ensure a well-informed press that was not the maidservant of the government. But *Le Monde* itself pointed out that the ideological position of the right-wing *L'Aurore* and that of the communist *L'Humanité* was bound to be at odds on this issue too.

Such a difference of view is at least characteristic of the wide political spectrum in Paris papers, and in the numerically far more significant provincial press. *Le Monde*, whose circulation is over 400 000 (50 000 more than *The Times*), is the only paper of real influence, but the Paris dailies include, besides *L'Aurore* and *L'Humanité*: two popular right-wing papers, *Le Parisien Libéré* (whose circulation of 783 000 owes much to its twenty different editions in the Paris region) and *France-Soir* (727 000); *Le Figaro*, a quality conservative Catholic paper (402 000); *La Croix*, Christian (130 000); and *Le Quotidien de Paris*, the vaguely-left successor of *Combat*. A far-left daily, *Libération*, started up in 1973.

France is too large a country geographically for a daily newspaper to achieve nationwide distribution and still be topical. This helps explain why *Le Monde* is to Fleet Street's eyes more of a daily weekly than a news daily; others concerned less with topicality than with depth and accuracy find it the best newspaper in the world. As in the United States, the lack of a full-blown national press leaves a big market for the news and opinion weeklies. *L'Express*, the reformist news magazine, has a circulation of 600 000, and the rival, *Le Point*, a little more conservative and started in 1972, already has a circulation of 164 000. The left-inclined *Le Nouvel Observateur* has almost 300 000. *Le Canard Enchaîné*, which never carries advertising, is sensationally well-informed and uncovered scandal after scandal under the Pompidou regime; it also writes about business misdeeds sooner than other papers. *Charlie Hebdo* is an anarchist mocker of everything and everyone. *Minute* is a vituperative right-wing weekly which is often well-informed. And there are many more. The anti-establishment press read by the establishment has its original home in Paris.

The only evidence of an upmarket bias in the press, of a quest for the business reader, comes in some of the weeklies. It is evident in the many management magazines aimed at business readers and at upper managers, in the 'cadres supérieurs'; the same general influence presumably had its part in the redirection in the format and content of *L'Express* which took place some years ago. But in the daily press advertisements do not cost more because the readership is of a higher income group. In fact in late 1974 it cost more to take a page advertisement in *L'Humanité* – £2·24 per thousand readers – than it did in *Le Monde* – £1·55 per thousand, for an admittedly smaller page size.

Advertising space is not usually sold by the newspapers themselves but through special space-selling agencies. The state-controlled advertising agency, Agence Havas, owns the biggest and is thus in the powerful position of both buying and selling advertisements. Publicis is another advertising agency that sells space under another hat. There is rarely any criticism of Havas or Publicis in the press. Nor much of Hachette, the giant publishing group with a finger in many pies, one being control of the monopoly that distributes magazines and newspapers in France. It also owns *France-Soir* and its Sunday version *Le Journal du Dimanche*. The instant success of *Le Point*, which it also owns, had something to do with Hachette's distribution power – though it was also due to the series of interviews that Gaullist ministers gave to it which they would not give to Jean-Jacques Servan-Schreiber's *L'Express*. In general, the press is owned by press people rather than by industrialists. *Le Monde* is 49 per cent owned by its journalists and workers.

The press in Germany is more regional and more wealthy but covers a smaller spectrum of opinion than the press in France. German publishers told the government in March 1974 that they were facing severe difficulties because of rising prices and falling advertising revenues and asked for greater indirect government aids. The chancellor at the time, Willy Brandt, was sympathetic and set up an inquiry. But chancellor Helmut Schmidt was less concerned, and a press bill was still at the talking stage towards the end of 1974.

The regional press in most countries has been doing well, and Germany's regional press has been no exception. German readers are conservative and parochial: a survey showed that while 60 per cent of the readers read the general political pages of their newspapers, 84 per cent read the regional and local pages. National news is covered extensively on television. Both major channels run four news broadcasts each evening and have a heavy dose of political magazine programmes and talk shows. Key Bundestag debates are broadcast in full.

The only mass circulation daily is Axel Springer's *Bild Zeitung*, whose blood and boobs style has built up a circulation of four million from its base in Hamburg. The profits more than offset losses of about £4 million a year on Springer's serious and right-wing *Die Welt*, which has a circulation of 231 000. (It is an interesting reflection of the common problems of quality-type newspapers that, of the four papers that join forces once a month to produce the hybrid *Europa*, *The Times*, *Die Welt* and *La Stampa* make losses and only *Le Monde* makes a profit. Perhaps there is a moral there in journalist-participation.) Springer also has a string of regional newspapers and controls 23 per cent of the daily newspaper market. He is Germany's only real press baron, and he owns and controls his empire himself.

The other papers that can aspire to national status are, like *Die Welt*, serious ones. *Frankfurter Allgemeine Zeitung* is a solid right-of-centre publication with a circulation of 278 000. There is a parallel with Britain's left-of-centre *Guardian*: 51 per cent is in the hands of a trust, to keep it pure, and 25 per cent is owned by a publisher that produces the downmarket local Frankfurt papers that bring in the money. Its circulation has risen in recent years while that of *Die Welt* has fallen. Two smaller papers have a growing national reputation: the liberal *Suddeutsche Zeitung* (Munich, 291 000), and the *Frankfurter Rundschau* (165 000), which owes its national circulation to a fair, left-of-centre reportage which makes it unique as a national paper. For the same reasons of geography as in France, the weekly newspapers and magazines like *Die Zeit*, *Der Spiegel* and *Stern* have a wide following.

The towering figure of Axel Springer is the bogeyman; he is held out as an example of the evils of concentrated press power. Press mergers and local monopolies have been the most immediate sign of the economic difficulties affecting the previously profitable regional newspaper. In mid-1974 the *Stuttgarter Zeitung* took over its rival the *Stuttgarter Nachrichten*, and in September the powerful *Westdeutsche Allgemeine Zeitung* (Essen, 754 000) announced that it was taking over another local paper, with a circulation of 223 000. However, in August the cabinet considered a draft amendment to the monopolies legislation that would make mergers between newspaper publishing houses with a combined annual turnover of £6 million subject to approval by the authorities. Similarly, in Britain, press mergers have to be referred to the Monopolies and Mergers Commission.

Germany has rather fewer direct or indirect aids to the press than other countries. Value Added Tax is levied, albeit at half the 11 per cent rate levied on other goods. The reduction in postal rates is mainly of benefit for delivering a small number of copies to a multitude of rural areas. A series of special loan funds which encourage the introduction of new machinery have, however, been very useful. Since labour problems on the British scale are unthinkable in Germany, newspapers have found it worthwhile to borrow and install modern equipment. The inquiry initiated by Brandt recommended that the newspapers publish rather more information about their plight before the government should take it seriously, but held out the prospect of a larger soft-loans fund. That such a basically prosperous industry should propose, and expect, government handouts may seem surprising to those in Britain who think of Germany as the modern home of unsupported free enterprise.

The trend towards press concentration of ownership is very marked in Holland. In the ten years to 1974, the number of newspaper publishers has fallen from fifty-two to twenty-nine, and the top four account for half the national and local newspaper sales. But there are still ten national and one hundred local papers, which is a lot for a country of thirteen million people. The standard European concessions on Value Added Tax and of reduced postal rates do not discriminate between the relatively weak and the relatively strong, so the strong benefit most. There has been a growing realization that some form of discriminatory aid is necessary to maintain diversity in the press, and a press fund to aid ailing papers was set up in September 1974. It is financed by a 5 per cent levy on radio and television advertising (the introduction of which was blamed for most of the problems of the press) which brings in almost £1 million a year. Money from the fund was offered to keep *De Tijd*, one of Holland's oldest papers, alive but its owners, the giant VNU publishing group, decided to transform it from a daily to a weekly.

The minister of culture, recreation and social work, whose responsibilities include the mass media, decides on applications to use the fund, on the advice of a committee. Publishers have to put forward a plan showing that a return to profitability is likely within a reasonable period. Fears that this will undermine the independence of papers is muted since journalists themselves have a strong say in most papers on the appointment of editors and on policy. The rescue fund is meant to be a temporary measure until the government has decided on a comprehensive plan for all the mass media. The government is committed to ensuring the survival of enough newspapers to give expression to the views of the major opinion groups in the country.

7 Remedies

The successful magazine writers are those who follow the taste of the class to whom they speak, in any aberration (fad, mannerism, or misapprehension) and in any shortcoming of insight or force which may beset that class.

Thorstein Veblen, *The Theory of Business Enterprise.*

Can the state subsidize its professional critics without emasculating them? Should the state legislate for weak newspapers to be supported by strong ones, or by a tax on advertising? If, as we argue, newspaper economics reinforce the inherent tendency of the serious press to direct its appeal to readers in the top socio-economic classes, will a scheme to help offset this distortion create evils worse than the complaint? We freely admit that it is easier to diagnose the problems of the press than to prescribe reforms. Any remedy requiring government action raises the spectre of government interference with the freedom of the press. As the functions and functionaries of the state multiply, and as a growing proportion of national income is spent or regulated by government departments and nationalized industries, it becomes ever more important that the press stay strong, independent of official control and free to criticize public authority in all its forms. But the matter cannot be left there, as it usually is. It is also important that the press use its freedom from state interference to apply its critical faculties to all the forces that shape society, including those that bolster the prosperity of the press. The press

E

is part of the dialogue of democracy, and as such has a constitutional role.

The press has no economic safeguard to ensure that it can carry
out this constitutional role other than its profits and the funds
of its owners. On the surface, profit makes a newspaper the master
of its own destiny. A profitable newspaper can publish and be
damned, it can be sued or be attacked by politicians and still
appear on the newsstands the next day. Newspapers must earn
their editorial freedom through profit, but not all means of
exercising such freedom are consistent with making a profit.
Avoidance of state interference helps ensure this limited freedom –
the freedom to go in certain directions only. Fully effective
freedom would require in addition a deliberate correction to the
normal play of market influences.

Profitability is an excellent criterion for many enterprises, both
private and state. The second best things in life are not free and
if people refuse to pay enough to the manufacturer of a brand of
soap suds to ensure his survival, then he should go out of business
and not waste the nation's resources. But a newspaper is not just
another brand of soap. This view is not just that of outside critics.
It has long been recognized by newspaper proprietors themselves.
Few of them have been in it for the money alone.

In most press groups, the criterion of 'profit – or death' is
suspended because one newspaper cross-subsidizes another, or
the profits from quite different activities subsidize the loss-
making newspapers. The *Sunday Telegraph* does not make a
profit; it is carried by *The Daily Telegraph*. *The Times* does not
make a profit; its losses have been set against profits from other
of Lord Thomson's activities, and have built up his moral credit
with establishment opinion. The *Daily Mail* does not make a
profit; it is cross-subsidized by Associated Newspapers' regional
newspapers, and may be later by its North Sea oil interests. *The
Guardian* does not make a profit; but the *Manchester Evening News*
carries it. The *Daily Express* makes a large loss in some years
and is kept alive by other newspapers in the Beaverbrook stable
and by its bankers who have the solid security of property in
Fleet Street to fall back on. If each newspaper had to stand or

fall on its own commercial merits, four out of the eight national dailies in late 1974 would cease publication.

Although so many newspapers are kept going by the munificence of their owners and their readiness to use other sources of income to cross-subsidize them, the belief that an unprofitable newspaper is an unwanted one is deeply ingrained. Profitability depends partly on managerial efficiency and editorial flair – but mostly on the place in the economic spectrum that the newspaper is occupying. The 1966 Economist Intelligence Unit report typifies the attitude: 'profits are not everything, but the lack of profits usually reflects other vices . . . no one would suggest that profits should be the only criterion, but an inefficient industry is usually an unhealthy industry'. The link is automatically made from unprofitability to inefficiency. Of course, if Fleet Street as a whole were more efficient, it would raise its collective profitability. But on individual titles the lack of profits may be due simply to the relatively low advertising revenue, which is related only haphazardly to the efficiency of a newspaper's management or to the quality of its editorial content.

The acceptance of profit as the criterion for newspapers is nowhere stronger than in Fleet Street itself. As that worldly newspaper boss and politician *manqué*, Cecil King, put it in his lecture on the 'Future of the Press,'[1] delivered in the same year that the EIU report reported on its present: 'We may resent the fact that newspapers, if they are to sell at a price which most people will pay, require big circulations in order to attract sufficient advertising; but then we have to reflect that advertising is a necessity of our mass production: mass consumption system; that it was created not by newspapers but by commerce.' For the upmarket press, these are the non-facts of economic life: these papers do not require big circulations; they require small, affluent ones. As a result, the range of opinion expressed in the existing choice of newspapers is too narrow and it is extremely difficult to begin new newspapers. As the 1947 Royal Commission put it – 'the gap between the best of the quality newspapers and the general run of the popular press is too wide, and the number of papers of an intermediate type is too small'. That number has since fallen with the deaths of the *News Chronicle* and the *Daily Herald*. What can be done?

The simplest remedy might appear to be a straight government subsidy to all unprofitable newspapers. This approach would be wrong on several counts. In the first place, if the government provides finance to make up deficits, it is bound to inquire into the causes of those deficits, and, further, to seek to regulate the operations involved. Parliament would not likely be willing to subsidize a newspaper run as a staff benevolent association. Questions would be asked in Parliament about the sports editor's expenses, and the press would be under constant pressure to justify itself. The newspaper receiving the subsidy would either toe the line, or would aggressively pull on it, and either way would strain its credibility with its readers. Secondly, the government would presumably not be willing to meet the deficits of all newspapers, even with the power to regulate their costs. Some official in some government department would then make a report that such and such a newspaper deserves subsidy whereas so and so does not, and even a fair-minded minister will be in an invidious position when he has to make up his mind on the basis of his own prejudices and on official report. So the discretion afforded the government would open the way to government influence on what the press writes. Any general scheme for helping newspapers must – except in very special circumstances – be automatic and avoid the need for discrimination and choice by officials or ministers. Thirdly, unprofitable newspapers are no more likely to be good editorially than profitable newspapers are likely to be efficiently managed. There is no rigid connexion between profit, editorial worth and efficiency, but going bankrupt provides a healthy, if cruel, disposal chute for those newspapers that have lost their audience, their advertisers and their purpose. The chute should not be blocked by subsidies that simply make up deficits. The lack of profits and the fear of death induces repentance and rethinking on the part of journalists, workers and managements, perhaps enabling small steps to be taken towards sensible manning levels and wage rates. Fleet Street is grossly inefficient in some respects and behindhand in the introduction of new technology; a subsidy to the unprofitable might perpetuate this state of affairs. We regard these objections to generalized subsidies as decisive.

But we do not believe that any measures that have the effect of supporting financially weak newspapers are self-defeating, although this was the argument of both the Shawcross Commission and the Economist Intelligence Unit reports. They harped on the theme that the forces of competition, the cost structure and the nature of the business lead to the strong getting stronger and the weak weaker, with the inevitable result that the trend to fewer newspapers would continue. Those newspapers with circulations in the ascendant got the best of two worlds – increasing economies of scale on costs, and increasing advertising revenue as they could charge more for reaching a wider readership. They could afford to pay high rates to their workers which their less well-off competitors had to strain to match – a tactic used both by Northcliffe and Beaverbrook. They had more money to make themselves bigger, fatter, better and brighter than other papers and attract more and more advertising and readers away from them. The Shawcross Commission could find no solution to the inevitable demise of the weaker papers. Generalized subsidies were objectionable in themselves and would do nothing to change the relative competitive position of any newspaper. Thus it came up with the lame advice – it cannot be called a remedy – that newspapers should improve 'the quality of the management and editorial direction'. This is rather like telling a sick man to get well, and is especially unhelpful in the light of the Commission's own analysis that the seesaw would inevitably tilt in the direction of the strongest.

Nicholas Kaldor and Robert Neild, economists from Cambridge, proposed a sophisticated scheme to the Shawcross Commission designed to cope with the economic forces leading to concentration. The idea was to charge a levy on advertising revenue that became progressively steeper as circulations rose and to distribute the proceeds as a subsidy to the papers with smaller circulations, which were presumed to be the weaker newspapers. This would help to counter the cumulative success in getting advertising enjoyed by whatever newspapers were leading the field, as well as their other economies of scale. By linking the subsidy to a criterion (in this case, circulation) other than the financial condition of the paper, the scheme succeeded in avoiding the dangers to press freedom and press efficiency that a subsidy to unprofitable newspapers would involve. The scheme raised a difficult problem of equity: why should the newspapers with high circulations – the popular newspapers in a literal sense – be saddled with the cost of the subsidy, rather than the taxpayer? Lord Shawcross said that he liked the *Daily Express* and did not see why millions of readers like him should suffer from a policy that would restrict its circulation. The authors pointed out that they were trying to counteract a pronounced trend to monopoly and that if the growing circulation of the *Daily Express* was leading to the closure of other dailies, there would be anti-social effects, which should be dealt with in the interests of press diversity. This was the function of the levy: not merely to provide finance, but also to offset the economies of scale and thus discourage ever-growing circulations. Since it was the expansionist policies of the big press barons that were seen to lead to the annihilation of the papers with circulations in the medium range, the appropriate corrective was to penalize circulation growth over a certain 'social limit', which the authors suggested on the basis of their limited access to the figures might be two million, and to give the money to the papers unable to benefit from economies of scale.

A similar feeling that the press rich should help the harassed poor lay behind a scheme proposed to the Shawcross Commission by the Young Fabians. They focused on essentially the same problem as Kaldor and Neild, and proposed as a remedy a ceiling on the proportion of their space that newspapers would be allowed to use for advertising. A limit of 40 per cent was designed to induce the leading newspapers to increase their advertising rates, or to ration space, either of which would divert advertisers to other papers. One major flaw in the scheme was that the strong papers could simply increase their total sizes so as to accommodate the advertisers within the limits set, and this would intensify the competition faced by the other papers.

When newspaper revenue exceeds the costs, the profits can be extremely large; when it does not, so can the losses be. Kaldor and Neild attempted to change the newspaper law that nothing succeeds like success by reducing the bonus of declining costs and increasing advertising revenue as circulation rose; and the Young Fabians tried to do the same by limiting the advertising bonus. Another scheme was proposed by *The Guardian* in 1966. Since very high profits have in the past accompanied very big circulations or very big paging, the latter largely representing volume of advertising, the simplest measure of economic success was tonnage of newsprint used. A newsprint levy was therefore proposed rising with the tonnage used; as in the Kaldor and Neild scheme such a levy was designed to help offset the economies of scale. It would reduce the profits per extra page of advertising carried. The money would be repaid to all newspapers on the basis of the editorial matter published, measured in square inches for all copies sold. In this way the heavy burden of first-copy editorial and production costs for a low circulation paper would be lightened; the net benefit would be greatest for papers with little advertising, smaller circulations and most editorial. This ingenious scheme, which was frankly designed to save *The Guardian* from the collapse that then seemed imminent, was put privately to Harold Wilson, as prime minister in 1966, but the Labour government refused to back this or any other scheme unless so requested by the Newspaper Publishers Association. Naturally the opposition of the newspapers that would be net losers squashed this levy subsidy scheme; no scheme where there are any predictable net losers can be introduced voluntarily.

Remedies designed to mitigate the rewards flowing to those at the winning end of the circulation stakes now appear in a different and less favourable light in view of the losses suffered by newspapers once considered strong. In the early 1960s, the reformers were after the *Daily Express*, the big spender with the booming circulation forcing its weaker competitors to match its size and wage rates. Ironically, the *Express's* boom ended in 1961 while the Shawcross Commission was sitting. For the newspapers that survived – eight dailies and seven Sundays in

1974 – circumstances have changed since the days when prosperity was simply a function of circulation. The thinning out of newspapers has left the survivors filling a series of niches, and there are few enough papers per niche for nearly all of them to survive – unless there is a general economic collapse. The product differentiation between the newspapers is considerable and each of them can count on a fair bit of brand loyalty. They do not have to watch each other's cover prices like hawks any more; there are even long stretches of time when close competitors have different prices.

If the newspaper market is a series of overlapping segmented markets rather than one big homogeneous one, then several consequences flow. The survival of the existing number of newspapers should be better assured than it has been in the past since the competition within each segment is less likely to lead to extinction than if each title was competing directly with all the others. Any remedies based on taking advantages away from some newspapers to help others – like those discussed above – are less appropriate, for in a segmented market the strength of one newspaper is less likely to be the cause of another's weakness; the cumulative forces favouring the strong and debilitating the weak will be less intensive. The fate of the *Daily Mail* is only distantly related to that of *The Sun*, and *The Guardian's* advertising poverty is not the victim of the affluence of the *Financial Times*. The *Mail* does have to worry about its near neighbour, the *Express*, and *The Guardian* about *The Times*.

Another important consequence of segmentation would be that reform proposals which have the effect of cutting the costs of all newspapers or of increasing all their revenues cannot be shot down on the grounds that they will not work because they leave the relative competitive positions of all newspapers unchanged. Much complacency among unions and managements has come from the fatalistic conclusions of the Shawcross Commission and of the Economist Intelligence Unit report that though it would be desirable for newspapers to be produced more economically, and to have higher revenues, this would not prevent the squeeze on whichever newspaper was then the weakest. Any improvement in its own position could quickly be undone by a similar improvement enjoyed by its strongest rivals, which would then capture more of the available sales and advertising revenue. But in a segmented market what one producer gains another need not lose. Gains in efficiency can help the industry as a whole; and so can support from government – though for the reasons discussed above there are decisive arguments against any subsidy that allows or obliges governments to discriminate between one paper and another and/or reduces the incentive for newspapers to improve their own financial lot.

As shown in Chapter 6, many other European countries give the press concessions of one form or another that decrease their costs or increase their revenues. Britain has become the exception rather than the rule in treating newspapers as a business just like any other. The one concession is that newspapers are zero-rated for Value Added Tax, which means they can reclaim the tax charged but do not have to charge it.

The most useful indirect help the British government could give would be to participate in a redundancy scheme, on the lines of that applied in the docks, to help newspapers help themselves and reduce manning levels. A more radical proposal voiced from time to time from the left is that the government should provide printing presses for rent to independent groups publishing their own newspapers and sharing the overhead costs. A facility of this kind would help new and small newspapers cut costs but it would have great practical difficulties, and give governments an undue influence over the press. Such influence might indeed be especially likely to be exercised against the kind of groups making the proposal.

Calls to subsidize newsprint have been frequently made. Newsprint is the largest cost item in newspaper budgets after wages; national newspapers spent about £150 million on newsprint in 1974. The newsprint price rise was partly the result of a deliberate policy by producers not to lay down enough capacity to cope with demand, so that a subsidy would mean that the government picked up the tab for a successful cartel arrangement. A flat subsidy would be more valuable to a popular newspaper, using thousands of tons of newsprint, than to a quality newspaper. A sliding scale would meet some of the snags but not all.

To sum up on the main proposals made in the past, government subsidies given directly to unprofitable newspapers would undermine the independence and efficiency of the press. Statutory measures that would penalize some newspapers in order to help others are based on a theory that there is an inherent tendency towards monopoly among newspapers – but this cannot entirely be borne out in practice any longer. Government aid that would apply to all newspapers indiscriminately might be of some use – and the rest of Europe has several ideas which are worth following up.

The proposals to which we now turn have as their object the creation of a more representative press, both by removing some of the constraints imposed by the economic struggle for survival and by making it easier for new newspapers to get off the ground. The principle of insulating the media from at least some commercial pressures in the interest of high standards is as old as the British Broadcasting Corporation. The Independent Broadcasting Authority ensures that the commercial television channel is not entirely filled with commercial pap.

The goal of a more representative press underlay a Labour Party discussion paper, 'The People and the Media', published in mid-1974. The means proposed are, however, open to severe objection. They fail the test that inducements for a better balance in the press must not reduce its independence from government interference. The intention was to move to a state of affairs 'where no distinction was made between readers in terms of their class, wealth and spending power'. This laudable object was to be achieved in an unlaudable way. Newspapers would be free to carry advertising, and advertisers would be free to determine the papers in which their advertisements were to go, but the money from the ads would be collected by an advertising revenue board, which would also determine advertising rates and would consider 'how best' to redistribute it. The board would charge high rates for advertisers wishing to reach small élite advertisers, but the newspapers would be deprived of the economic benefit of having a small élite readership. Revenue returned to newspapers would be related to the size of their readership, rather than to size and composition. Thus the facts of life which let the *Financial Times* make a profit with a fraction of the circulation of the old *Daily Herald*'s would be overruled by administrative decision.

The distribution of advertising revenue in proportion to readership would not be a precise criterion, as part of the proceeds of the levy would be used for a differential newsprint subsidy to help small circulation papers, and another part for grants to a development fund for the launch of new papers. Considerable discretionary power would remain with the board. A non-elected body would be given a fundamental – and dangerous – political role of determining how much money each press group could make. The board's officials would also be faced with the Solomon-like task of determining what advertising rates different newspapers should charge in conditions in which newspapers had lost the incentive to get advertising revenue.

It would be possible to devise a scheme that 'democratized' newspaper readers and gave each of them the same weight no matter what their socio-economic group. A levy could be charged on those newspapers able to charge advertisers over the odds, i.e. that had above-average millinch rates, to be distributed to papers with below-average rates. This would avoid the need for discretionary decisions, but the practical difficulties would be enormous.

Our own proposal is therefore grounded on the following basic principles: no sticks, small carrots to those that want to eat them, financed by the taxpayer and set according to an objective formula. The proposal is directed at a limited but important aim: to encourage papers with relatively small circulations to look more to the number of their readers and less to their class and their incomes; and to give this encouragement in particular to new newspapers.

The core of the proposal that we put forward is for a small-circulation cash bounty. The bounty would be payable not on circulation itself but on increases in circulation.

If a newspaper succeeded in increasing its circulation by 100 000 – in accordance with the rules of the scheme as detailed below – and the bounty was, say, £10 per extra sale, which compares with the £16 that a daily newspaper costing 8p gets from a reader in a year – it would in the relevant year receive a bounty of £1 million. This sum should come out of the public purse since the object of the scheme is the public interest one of increasing the diversity of the press. There is no reason why profitable newspapers should pay the costs of such a scheme – unless it can be shown that their profits directly cause the losses of other newspapers. Neither should the scheme be funded out of a tax on, say, advertising; such a tax may or may not be justifiable in its own right – but the temptation to kill too many birds with one stone should be resisted. If better newspapers are in the public interest, then the public should pay for them via general taxation.

To qualify for the small circulation bounty, a newspaper would have to have had an average paid daily circulation over three years of a minimum of 50 000 and a maximum of one million. The minimum is set high enough to ensure that a newspaper has established a firm base of public demand, but low enough to allow new newspapers to qualify in the early years of their existence. If a new newspaper passed the qualifying limit and increased its circulation by 10 000 in a year, it would get a bounty of £100 000. This sort of financial inducement is a better way of encouraging new newspapers than handing out cash grants in advance of proof that it can attract readers. The bounty will begin to tail off when advertising revenue is 65 per cent of the total (excluding bounty) and reduce to zero at 75 per cent. Newspapers in this band would have a special incentive to go further downmarket than would otherwise be profitable.

The circulation maximum reflects the fact that at a certain level of circulation, a newspaper begins to benefit from economies of scale, being able to spread its fixed costs over a large number of readers. We have tentatively fixed this level at one million, but this would have to be reviewed in the light of more information as well as new production techniques.

The scheme should initially be limited to daily newspapers but could be expanded to the Sundays and weeklies and to local papers with a circulation under 50 000 if it proved successful. Our scheme does not differentiate between national newspapers and regional ones, and the *Birmingham Post* and *The Scotsman* would both qualify. This would help any newspaper with ambitions to follow the trail blazed by the *Manchester Guardian* to national status. Once a newspaper had been included, no extra discretionary judgements would have to be made. There would be no interference by the government or by any other body; operation would be automatic and non-selective.

The only judgement would be in defining what counted as a newspaper. This should not be a demanding task as long as the scheme was limited to dailies. The element of discretion would increase once it were extended to papers appearing only once a week – including Sunday papers. This one necessary judgement in the scheme should be made by a body independent of the government and also relatively well informed about the press. The most suitable composition seems to us to be the chairman of the Press Council together with its lay members – but not its press representatives. This body should make its judgement according to the following broad guideline – that a substantial proportion of the newspaper's coverage be devoted to serious reporting and discussion of national affairs. Some local evening papers like London's *Evening Standard* would qualify. The council would also prevent cheating by splitting a paper into regional editions with circulations each under the one million mark. The secretariat of the Press Council would be the right body to administer the scheme, which would involve processing the applications for bounty, checking that the sales figures were audited and then doing the computations and sending out the cheques.

To guard against short-lived promotional bursts which boost the circulation for long enough to get bounty, three-year rolling averages should be used as a basis for computation except in the case of new newspapers which should qualify as soon as the average of 50 000 is reached for a three-year period. The bounty for 1974 would be based on the increase in the average daily circulation of the three years 1972, 1973 and 1974 over that of 1969, 1970 and 1971; the bounty for 1975 would be based on the increase in the average daily circulation of 1973, 1974 and 1975 over that of 1970, 1971 and 1972, and so on. There would be no repayment if circulation was falling instead of rising.

Had such a scheme been working during the period in which *The Times* was trying to increase its circulation (see p. 79), the bounty payments would have gone some way towards meeting the heavy promotional expenses. Through the early 1960s, the circulation was stuck at around 255 000, but in 1966 the circulation rose by 28 000. The circulation in each of 1964 and 1965 was 256 000 and the average for the three years 265 000; the average for the base period 1961 to 1963 was 254 000 and so the bounty would have been 265 000 minus 254 000 times £10, or £110 000. The Thomson Organization then bought *The Times* and intensified the sales drive and the circulation grew by leaps and bounds to 394 000 in 1967, 408 000 in 1968 and a peak of 432 000 in 1969. The bounty payments accruing to *The Times* would have been £$\frac{1}{2}$ million, £1 million and £1$\frac{1}{2}$ million in those years. This would have helped offset the adverse effect on advertising revenue of the dilution in the readership profile that the increase in circulation involved. As it was, this dilution helped persuade *The Times* management to reverse tack.

As indicated the bounty would begin to tail off when advertising income is 65 per cent of the total. The *Financial Times*, which in 1973 got about 80 per cent of its revenue from advertising, would not get any bounty in normal times – but it would if there was an advertising recession while its circulation was rising. One of the side advantages of the small circulation bounty is that it operates in a counter-cyclical way, smoothing out the impact of the ups and downs of business.

It might be objected that the bounty is élitist: it would give money to *The Guardian* but not to the *Daily Mail* although both make losses. The scheme does indeed deliberately concentrate on the élitist papers – with the avowed aim of reducing one of the major economic forces leading to élitism; it tries to make up for the fact that in the eyes of the advertiser one reader is not worth as much as another by giving a classless cash bounty for all extra readers. The incentive is quite a strong one. Since the £10 does not have any costs attached, the strategy of going for circulation may become a feasible proposition for a quality paper.

The bounty is not a generalized subsidy designed to put money into the cash boxes of all newspapers. It is designed to help newspapers in a specific situation, as measured objectively by their circulation, the increase in their circulation, and the proportion of their revenue derived from advertising. Newspapers as a whole do not want generalized subsidies, nor do they need them in normal times. When the times are abnormal, say during superinflation or depression, then newspapers may need special temporary assistance like industry as a whole. The small-circulation bounty is not suitable for use as an emergency rescue operation for newspapers in general or for particular titles. An important argument for its introduction is that it should make both these alternative forms of support less necessary, though they can probably never be ruled out. The availability of the bounty would also be a small help to papers with competent management and editorial direction to raise funds from brokers and bankers.

If a profitable newspaper gets bounty, this will be a direct indication of its efficiency, and it will deserve support. Part of the bounty will in any case be clawed back by the Exchequer since bounty will count as taxable revenue; if a newspaper is making a trading loss of £300 000 and gets bounty of £400 000, it will pay tax on the profit of £100 000.

The usual objection to schemes that attempt to interfere with the free market is that they are impractical. That cannot be said of the bounty. Exact figures of circulation are available from the Audit Bureau of Circulation. The basis for computation is simple. The advertising cut-off provision is straightforward. Any point that needs arbitration could be resolved by the Press Council committee. No newspaper would be obliged to join the bounty scheme; if it wants to fly the flag of purity, money would not be forced upon it. It is unlikely that the annual demands on the Treasury would fluctuate by wild amounts. The extra secretariat staff needed by the Press Council to cope with administration would be tiny – and some of the information collection should be done anyway by the Press Council, one of whose neglected tasks is to keep a watching brief on the finances of the press.

The most serious objection to the small-circulation bounty is that it could be the thin end of the wedge of government interference: the use of government money as a partial corrective to the necessity to get advertising money will in this view introduce a bias of its own. That is an argument for accepting the marketplace with all its limitations as the lesser of two evils. But we believe that the forces of the market can be counterbalanced by government without diminishing their beneficial impact, and without opening the way to direct government interference.

It is the natural instinct of editors and circulation managers to broaden the circulation of their newspapers. But for the quality press the economics of the advertising connexion makes a representative readership a financial millstone. As the 1947 Royal Commission put it, a newspaper 'sells its space in a buyer's market and therefore has a considerable inducement to adopt a tone which will cause advertisers to regard it as a good advertising medium'. For the mass circulation newspapers, the bigger the mass, the better off the paper as a medium for advertisers and the more economical its production, since it can spread costs over a very large number. For the papers with circulations in the hundreds of thousands rather than millions, the economics of large scale operation hardly begin to operate, but their costs of production are already heavy. They are therefore obliged to consider the attractiveness of their readers to potential advertisers, since advertising pays the bills. They may decide to ignore the results of such an analysis; to publish and be shunned. But there is a strong economic pressure on small circulation papers, which are the ones that carry weight in public debate, to aim at the readers in the A and B socio-economic groups, and to be the upmarket press. This may well be their target audience in any case. But for the newspaper that wants its message to carry to a wider readership, for the newspaper that would like to drop out of the consensus of opinion that characterizes the quality press, and for the new newspaper that wants to break into the small circle, the path has been blocked. The small-circulation bounty takes a few of the brambles out of the way.

The advertising connexion is not the only commercial pressure on the press, and neither are commercial pressures the only ones that determine the shape of the press. Britain's tight libel laws and strict rules on contempt of court, the tradition of closed government, the views of some proprietors, the social background of journalists and a whole host of other factors have exerted their influences on the press. What we hope to have achieved in this short book is to turn attention to a neglected one: the economic pressure on the serious press to be the upmarket press.

Reference

1 KING, Cecil, *The Future of the Press*, MacGibbon and Kee, 1967, page 73.

Appendix

Newspaper profit and loss accounts

The national newspaper industry has a small number of products (eight dailies, seven Sundays) and an even smaller number of companies (nine) that publish them. With such a small but varied collection of companies, aggregated statistics do not provide sufficient material for an understanding of the structure of the industry. We sought to get detailed figures from the nine, and succeeded with three of them.

The figures are drawn unadjusted from the companies' own accounting systems, and as these systems are never alike, the figures are not fully comparable. The classification of revenue caused least problems. Of the three IPC newspapers, the *Daily Mirror* gets less than a fifth of its advertising revenue from classifieds, and the others hardly any, and so we have not given a breakdown of advertising for them. Circulation revenue is that actually received by the papers, i.e. after deduction of the 35 per cent newsagents' discount; and display advertising revenue is after the agencies' 15 per cent commission.

The direct costs – which form the basis for the table on page 62 – are those that can be allocated to a department or cost centre. Newsprint includes ink, except in the case of Times Newspapers. Editorial costs are largely the wages, travel and expenses of journalists, and the wages of sub-editors and ancillary departments. Production costs are from the five main production departments: Composing, where the copy is set and the pages made up; Process, where photographs are made into blocks; Foundry, where printing cylinders are made up from pages; Machine Room, where the printing is done; Publishing, where the papers are bundled up and despatched. Distribution is the cost of transport from Fleet Street to the newspaper wholesalers.

Selling is the cost of the advertising department, and of promoting the paper.

Allocatable overheads refer to those costs which can be assigned to a paper in a group, but not to a particular department. The excess of revenue over direct costs and allocatable overheads is the trading profit of each paper – but the profit of the group of which the paper forms a part is struck after interest charges and other central charges, and crediting income from other sources – for example, The Times atlases. IPC Newspapers do not allocate overheads between papers, and so the surplus over costs, which in IPC's case we have called the trading *surplus*, cannot be directly compared with the trading *profit* on other newspapers. Times Newspapers gave us the figures for two recent years but not a run of years. For the table on page 62, *The Sunday Times* Magazine's figures have been added to those of the main paper.

Financial Times Years to December 31

	1966	1970	1971	1972	1973
Revenue £000s					
Advertisement:					
Display	3 502	5 480	6 258	8 302	9 277
Classified	380	758	933	1 348	1 857
	3 882	6 238	7 191	9 650	11 134
Circulation	850	1 633	1 893	2 390	2 569
Other*	104	115	153	126	118
	4 836	7 986	9 237	12 166	13 821
Costs £000s					
Newsprint	493	893	979	1 194	1 444
Production	1 178	2 124	2 539	2 982	3 770
Distribution	456	730	760	1 023	1 242
Editorial	726	1 325	1 609	1 853	2 154
Selling	416	779	1 093	1 234	1 343
	3 269	5 851	6 980	8 286	9 953

Allocatable overheads	521	932	1 119	1 520	1 626
	3 790	6 783	8 099	9 806	11 579
Trading profit £000s	1 046	1 203	1 138	2 360	2 242
Circulation 000s	152	174	168	188	194
Average paging	24·4	32·3	33	36	38·7
Advertising content %	41	42	42	45	46
Editorial employees	193	250	259	274	298†
Production employees	380	501	564	567	574

* Mostly rent received.
† Of which 200 are journalists.

IPC Newspapers   Years to end March
Daily Mirror

	1966	1971	1972	1973	1974
Revenue £000s					
Advertisement	8 142	9 104	9 918	10 449	12 343
Circulation	16 547	21 475	24 613	25 140	26 947
Other	85	–	–	–	–
	24 774	30 579	34 531	35 589	39 290
Costs £000s					
Newsprint	6 962	7 506	8 788	9 010	11 657
Production	4 392	5 745	6 508	7 113	8 376
Distribution	1 242	1 814	2 275	2 639	3 057
Editorial	1 814	3 155	3 517	3 911	4 422
Selling	370	1 006	2 020	1 627	1 648
	14 780	19 226	23 108	24 300	29 160

Trading surplus

£000s	9 994	11 353	11 423	11 289	10 130

Circulation, 000s	5 003	4 450	4 353	4 274	4 286
Average paging	26	29	30	32	31
Advertising content %	36	35	34	36	39

Sunday Mirror
Revenue £000s

Advertisement	2 390	2 786	3 209	3 215	3 616
Circulation	4 244	5 932	6 992	7 613	8 033
Other	7	–	–	–	–
	6 641	8 718	10 201	10 828	11 649

Costs £000s

Newsprint	1 736	2 187	2 386	2 452	3 122
Production	1 917	2 542	2 838	3 136	3 438
Distribution	402	728	850	1 005	1 275
Editorial	695	1 182	1 301	1 410	1 480
Selling	264	344	366	372	388
	5 014	6 983	7 741	8 375	9 703

Trading surplus

£000s	1 627	1 735	2 460	2 453	1 946

Circulation, 000s	5 067	4 726	4 629	4 493	4 575
Average paging	39	44	46	46	45
Advertising content %	39	39	42	42	43

Sunday People

Revenue £000s					
Advertisement	2 994	3 009	3 323	3 239	3 429
Circulation	4 644	6 288	7 178	7 623	7 615
Other	87	–	–	–	–
	7 725	9 297	10 501	10 862	11 044

Costs £000s					
Newsprint	2 228	2 475	2 569	2 542	3 086
Production	1 982	3 038	3 642	3 785	4 151
Distribution	477	926	927	1 026	1 214
Editorial	800	939	1 096	1 272	1 365
Selling	469	363	487	439	397
	5 956	7 741	8 721	9 064	10 213

Trading surplus £000s					
	1 769	1 556	1 780	1 798	831
Circulation 000s	5 535	5 008	4 767	4 478	4 406
Average paging	22	21	22	22	21†
Advertising content %	46	43	44	43	45

Group profit Trading					
surpluses	13 390	14 614	15 663	15 540	12 907
Indirect costs*	5 372	9 961	11 194	11 834	13 851
Trading profit/ (loss)	8 018	4 653	4 469	3 706	(944)

* Includes rent, rates, power, maintenance, administration, but excludes interest charges and depreciation.

† To Sept 1973; it then went tabloid.

Times Newspapers

Years to December 31

	The Times		The Sunday Times		The Sunday Times Magazine	
	1971	1973	1971	1973	1971	1973
Revenue £000s						
Advertisement:						
Display and financial	3 033	4 656	3 301	4 092	3 927	6 018
Classified	2 584	4 611	3 393	5 652	–	–
	5 617	9 267	6 694	9 744	3 927	6 018
Circulation	3 222	3 430	3 481	4 719	–	–
Other	41	76	62	77	–	–
	8 880	12 773	10 237	14 540	3 927	6 018
Costs £000s						
Newsprint	1 615	2 356	2 235	3 150	1 092	1 782
Production	3 021	4 218	3 124	4 477	1 522*	2 286*
Depreciation‡	187	176	254	298	–	–
Distribution	706	989	816	1 084	689†	868†
Editorial	2 414	2 551	1 679	1 705	354	433
Publicity (selling)	1 096	1 279	913	1 028	72	94
Redundancy payments‡	64	3	39	7	–	–

Allocatable overheads	9 103	11 572	9 060	11 749	3 729	5 463
	1 136	1 388	1 343	1 747	–	–
	10 239	12 960	10 403	13 496	3 729	5 463
Trading Profit (loss) £000s	(1 359)	(187)	(166)	1 044	198	555
Circulation 000s	340	345	1 418	1 516	–	–
Average paging	27·7	32·4	59	67·8	63·9	80·9
Advertising content %	35	42	57	59	57	58
Editorial employees	403	373	152	157	30	28
Production employees	1 065	1 001	800	815	–	–

* The Magazine is printed under contract by Sun Printers Ltd.

† Includes a special handling payment to wholesalers and retailers.

‡ Included with production for table 4.2 on page 62.

Times Newspapers made a profit from other activities, such as *The Times Literary* and *Educational Supplements*, of £459 000 in 1971 and £1 266 000 in 1973 after interest charges, so Times Newspapers made an overall loss of £868 000 in 1971 and a £2 678 000 profit in 1973.

Index